The Stone of Israel and the Two Witnesses

The Stone of Israel and the Two Witnesses

Destiny's Epilogue

Susan Alfson, Ph.D.

Writers Club Press
San Jose New York Lincoln Shanghai

The Stone of Israel and the Two Witnesses
Destiny's Epilogue

Writers Club Press
an imprint of iUniverse.com, Inc.

For information address:
iUniverse.com, Inc.
5220 S 16th, Ste. 200
Lincoln, NE 68512
www.iuniverse.com

ISBN: 0-595-15935-4

Printed in the United States of America

In loving memory of my mother, Marjorie Prees Alfson

Contents

Epigraph

"Joseph is a fruitful bough, even a fruitful bough by a well; whose branches run over the wall: The archers have sorely grieved him, and shot at him, and hated him: But his bow abode in strength, and the arms of his hands were made strong by the hands of the mighty God of Jacob: (from thence is the shepherd, the stone of Israel:) Genesis 49:22-24, AV.

Acknowledgements

I want to thank all of the scholars who helped make this book possible-Florentino García Martínez, for his diligent translation of the Dead Sea Scrolls; Yair Davidy, for his extensive research into lost Israelite identity; E. Raymond Capt and Artisan publishers, for archaeological and historical evidence, and; Bobby Rich, for information pertinent to the identity of the last prophet- Elijah. I also wish to thank Dr. Timothy Dawson for his financial support that helped to fund the research of this book.

Chapter One

Introduction to the Two Witnesses

"And I will give power unto my two witnesses, and they shall prophesy a thousand and threescore days, clothed in sackcloth. These are the two olive trees, and the two candlesticks standing before the God of the earth. And if any man will hurt them, he must in this manner be killed. These have power to shut heaven, that it rain not in the days of their prophecy: and have power over waters to turn them to blood, and to smite the earth with all plagues as often as they will."[1]

These are pretty strong words! So strong, in fact, that most religious leaders choose to shun this portion of the Bible. It is always easier to close your eyes to unpleasant truth, than it is to accept it. Besides, it is not politically correct in today's mainstream religion to delve into topics that are not considered "acceptable" Christianity. Many modern day ministers would dismiss this chapter of Revelation, as well as most of the rest of Revelation, as being symbolic and not to be taken literally. Or, they instruct their congregation not to worry about this portion of the Bible, because it pertains to the Jews, and they, as Christians, will be raptured before these things occur anyway. Not to worry! How wrong this is! These are the ministers of the gospel that Jesus said would arise in the last days and lead the elect astray, if that were possible. It will be

1

some of these same religious leaders who will demand the death of these two prophets, and will rejoice with the rest of the world when their executions are carried out.

Who are these two that step onto the stage of world history, with regal authority, seemingly out of oblivion? The clues are there for those with insight and inquisition that are willing to search the scriptures for answers. I have written this book for those not willing to go to such profound study. The grand finale of these two anointed ones is the next step in God's great drama and it is beneficial to learn something about them.

These two witnesses are anointed by God and are given awesome and tremendous responsibility in the last chapter of this age. First of all, they have a ministry to the nations. They are the last two prophets of God, and as such, they will come preaching a message of repentance. They will be heard loud and clear from God's holy city and pulpit, Jerusalem. Second, they will be dressed in sackcloth, as a sign of mourning, to give direction for others to follow their lead and repent of all the horrible sins that have been committed in the name of Jesus. Third, these two come to turn people from their complacency and spiritual indifference that has separated them from the face of God. These witnesses are not to be taken lightly because they come at a time of turbulence, chaos, and uncertainty to warn the world that the time has come to repent and be restored, so that the time of salvation can arrive. These are the last two prophets of God.[2] They will not and can not be subdued until their mission and time on earth is complete.

Prophecy is a gift from God. It is absolute and authoritative in the hands of these two prophets. Their words are irrefutable. What they say can not be withdrawn or recanted and because of this these two prophets must have complete control over their emotions and speech. Anything else would be a dangerous error on God's part. God must be absolutely sure of what he is doing to bestow this gift upon these two chosen prophets. They will torment a world bent on self-gratification and greed that has forgotten the path of righteousness and love. Most people will not challenge what they say, more out of fear than out of respect. But, these two prophets will understand the working of the minds of the wicked and they will be allowed to feel and see inside their thoughts. Many people will hide from this light for fear of being exposed and condemned. It will not be a pleasant time for the wicked.[3]

God gives these two witnesses power over the forces of nature comparable to the power that he gave Moses over nature. God gave Moses power to turn water into blood as well as control over the weather. He was also given authority to send plague after plague upon the kingdom of Pharaoh, because Pharaoh would not listen to Gods word, as it came through Moses, to let the children of Israel go and release them from their bondage. A similar time is fast approaching. These last two prophets will have all of these abilities and they will be coming in the power and spirit of Moses to seek freedom for the Israelites that are once again lost.

Moses, himself, spoke of Israel's coming deliverer. " The Lord thy God will raise up unto thee a Prophet from the midst of thee, of thy brethren, like unto me; unto him you shall hearken. And the Lord said unto me, They have well spoken that which they have spoken. I will raise them up a Prophet from among their brethren, like unto thee, and will put my words in his mouth; and he shall speak unto them all that I shall command him. And it shall come to pass, that whosoever will not hearken unto my words which he shall speak in my name, I will require it of him."[4] This refers to the Elijah to come who heralds in the approach, as one of them, of the two witnesses and the subsequent return of Jesus to rule this world.

The two witnesses will proclaim their God given message for three and one half years. After three and one half years of testimony, the beast will overpower and kill them. This is all within the divine plan of God. God will then withdraw his miraculous, supernatural protection because their prophetic, earthly appointment with destiny will have been fulfilled. After they die, they will be denied burial and their bodies will lie in the streets of Jerusalem. The people of the world will celebrate their deaths and sent each other gifts (peace offerings) in celebration of being released from the torment that was inflicted upon them in successive blows by these two intense and terrifying "madmen." What relief the world will experience. But just when things begin to get back to "normal," they will stand upon their feet.

"And after three days and an half the spirit of life from God entered into them, and they stood upon their feet; and great fear fell upon them which saw them, come up hither. And they ascended up to heaven in a cloud; and their enemies beheld them."[5]

So, now, we have a general picture of the two witnesses. First, they are sent to Jerusalem to speak the word of repentance to the nations. Second, God anoints them with power and authority. Third, they are inviolable for a time span of three and one half years. They can not be harmed or killed during the time of their testimony. If anybody tries to harm them, by the same token they will be destroyed. Fourth, they will have complete control over the forces of nature. They will have power to shut the heavens and prevent rain from falling. They will have power to turn waters to blood, and; they will have power to inflict plague and destruction as often as they are given direction from God to do so. Are you beginning to understand this picture? Why else do you suppose God sends them?

"And there was given me a reed like unto a rod: and the angel stood, saying, Rise, and measure the temple of God, and the altar, and them that worship therein."[6]

These two witnesses come to oversee the rebuilding of the third temple in Jerusalem. Contrary to what many Christians believe they do not come to condemn the Jews for their beliefs. On the contrary, these two are sent by God to make certain that this temple is built according to the specifications set forth in the Bible. The temple will be rebuilt and true temple worship will be restored in order to properly worship God and to prepare for the soon return of Jesus. The temple of King Solomon was destroyed in 587 BC.[7] This marked the end of the dynasty of King David in Jerusalem. King Zedekiah, of the lineage of David, was the last ruling King in this temple, in Jerusalem. These two anointed of God are going to restore the splendor and the kingdom of David to its rightful city as an offering to God.

Once the true temple and temple worship is restored, the glory of God will permeate Zion. Jerusalem will, once again, become a stumbling block to all those who oppose her. This small area will be a fortress of salvation and protection to those who long for it and to those to whom it belongs. This glorious city will become a blessing or a curse to the rest of the nations. The religious powers of the day will oppose this move by God. As the temple is restored, the remainder of the rightful heirs to the land will be summoned to return. The Jews, from the house of Judah, who are in Jerusalem at this time, are only one piece to the puzzle. The temple can not be rebuilt until these two witnesses are called forth and arrive on the scene to initiate the restoration of the kingdom.

The two witnesses arrive to convict the world of sin and lead them to repentance. These two come to show the world that they have sinned against God and against Jesus by so blatantly disregarding the statutes and the laws. They instruct the people of the world to repent because the temple is being rebuilt, and Jesus will soon come to rule as King of Kings, and Lord of Lords. The two witnesses are aware of their own sins and repent, in humility, as a witness to the world in preparation for the coming of Jesus. They are aware that this temple is sacred and nothing wicked will be allowed in it. Their message is one of contrition and restoration. As the temple is restored the sins of the people who come humbly to God seeking forgiveness will be removed. God is a merciful God who loves his creation. This will be mankind's last call to repentance before the final curtain of judgement begins to fall.

The two anointed and chosen witnesses will also be followers of Jesus who come to mend the breaches of the gospel and the pervasive misunderstandings that abound. As they preach the gospel of the kingdom, and of Jesus who is coming to reign, they will be opposed by the world system of belief. Some will even boldly attempt to stop them, but will be destroyed in their endeavor. Many so called "Christians", some sincere and others not so sincere, will try to stop the mission of these two witnesses of Jesus claiming that they are servants of the devil who have come to mislead and tempt true Christians. It will be "Christians" who demand their deaths claiming this move of God is a facade and blasphemy against Jesus. Some will even claim that these two are the antichrist and the false prophet that have come to deceive the world. The religious assumptions of the day will have been made a mockery of and these miracle workers of Satan must go! But, these are no miracle workers of Satan, rather; they are Gods anointed servants that are ordained to complete the epilogue of Gods history and to usher in the millennial rule of Jesus.

A great portion of the world will be set on edge by the conciliatory message of the kingdom that these two come to proclaim. Jesus came to expound on this kingdom and was crucified for his teaching. The earthly reign of Jesus has not yet begun, and his speaking in parables was a smokescreen that had prophetic significance for this endtime. The gospel of the kingdom was never totally understood, not even by the disciples of Jesus. It had to be that way because Jesus was only authorized to do what he was authorized to do. This is another mystery that has never been completely understood. The two anointed that come will be empowered to expound on the mystery surrounding Christ. Although the ushering in of this kingdom will be a wonderful time of peace and justice, the kingdoms of the world will not want change. They will have no desire to give up their leadership to a superior king and kingdom, even though they have so miserably failed in the responsibilities of this temporal world. It is because of this rebellious attitude that many people and nations will be destroyed in the period following the death of the two witnesses known as the "Great Tribulation."

This period will be the most horrific time since history began. There is nothing to compare it with. Because of humanity's rebellion, unwillingness to be under authority, and an inability to follow rules; they will reap what they have sown. It will be a gruesome picture- the prophesied Apocalypse. Those who heed the message of God's chosen delegates will be spared, protected, or they will die before this period of the greatest massacre, destruction, and hell that this world has ever experienced.[8]

In other places of the Bible, these two witnesses are referred to as two olive trees. They are the sons of oil. The Holy Spirit illuminates them with the oil of life and light. Although they are human, their power is supernatural. Zechariah explains this in more detail.

"Then answered I, and said unto him, What are these two olive trees upon the right side of the candlestick and upon the left side thereof? And I answered again, and said unto him, What be these two olive branches which through the two golden pipes empty the golden oil out of themselves? And he answered me and said, Knowest thou not what these be? And I said, No, my lord. Then said he, These are the two anointed ones, that stand by the Lord of the whole earth."[9]

Do you see the significance in this last sentence? The two witnesses are the two that are so close to Jesus that the three can not be separated. These are the two that stand by Jesus, one on the right, and one on the left when he comes to rule his kingdom. Jesus makes mention of these two in Matthew. A woman comes to Jesus and requests a favor: "Grant that these my two sons may sit, the one on thy right hand, and the other on the left, in thy kingdom."[10] Jesus made it very clear that it was not for him to decide.

"And he said unto them, Ye shall drink indeed of my cup, and be baptized with the baptism that I am baptized with: but to sit on my right hand, and on my left, is not mine to give, but it shall be given to them for whom it is prepared of my Father. [11]

The two anointed witnesses will be of Israelite origin. The house of Judah and the house of Israel separated into two kingdoms in 926 BC. Before this time, they were one kingdom under David, and then Solomon. After the reign of Solomon, the kingdoms separated.[12] Israel was scattered from this point forward with the children of Israel losing their identities. Some of Judah retained their identity. The two that are coming will be full-blooded Israelite. One of them will be of Judah from the lineage of Solomon, and the other one will be of the lineage of Nathan. When the hand of God authorizes these two, those seeking righteousness will recognize them. There will be no mistaking who these two are and the reason that they both were born.

God chose them from the womb.[13] They were handpicked to finish the work that Jesus started. Because of their own particular and unique Heritage, they are the culmination of all the Biblical promises from the Old forward into the New Testament. They are the gatherers. Jesus came to seek the lost sheep of Israel and to preach the gospel of the kingdom. These two witnesses will finish this ministry. They will restore the glory to Jerusalem. Isaiah 49 is in reference to one of these two witnesses.

"And now saith the Lord that formed me from the womb to be his servant, to bring Jacob again to him, Though Israel be not gathered, yet shall I be glorious in the eyes of the Lord, and my God shall be my strength. And he said, it is a light thing that thou shouldest be my servant to raise up the tribes of Jacob, and to restore the preserved of Israel: I will also give thee for a light to the gentiles, that thou mayest be my salvation unto the ends of the earth."[14] This is one of many chapters in the Bible that identifies a witness.

Haggai 2 is another chapter that portrays the other chosen one. "Speak to Zerubbabel, governor of Judah, saying I will shake the heavens and the earth; And I will overthrow the chariots, and those that ride in them; and the horses and their riders shall come down, every one by the sword of his brother. In that day sayeth the Lord of hosts, will I take thee, O Zerubbabel, my servant, the son of Shealtiel, saith the Lord, and will make thee a signet: for I have chosen thee, saith the Lord of hosts."[15] There can be no doubt; these two are God's chosen pillars.

These two pillars of God, as Jesus' witnesses, will be the only source of strength, light, and support for a dying world, during their three and one half year testimony. They will have all knowledge and wisdom to teach truth to a world hungry for knowledge at a time when all have gone astray and no one knows the way. These two will guide and show the way of righteousness to all that desire guidance. Listening and following these two prophets will mean the difference between life and death at the end of this age. This life or death choice will be an eternal one. It will mean the difference between being with God or being separated from him, sadly, ever after.

Chapter Two

Jacob's Pillar and Descendants

Let's start at the beginning with some relevant and pertinent history in order to get a grasp on the identities of these two approaching anointed witnesses. A good place to begin is in Genesis with the patriarch of Israel, Jacob. Jacob had a strange dream on one of his travels: "And Jacob went out from Beersheba, and lighted upon a certain place, and tarried there all night, because the sun was set; and he took of the stones of that place, and put them for his pillows, and lay down in that place to sleep. And he dreamed, and behold a ladder set up on the earth, and the top of it reached to heaven: And behold, the Lord stood above it, and said, I am the Lord God of Abrahamn thy father, and the God of Isaac: the land whereon thou liest, to thee will I give it, and to thy seed; And thy seed shall be as the dust of the earth, and thou shall spread abroad to the west, and to the east, and to the north, and to the south: And in thee and in thy seed shall all the families of the earth be blessed. And behold, I am with thee, and I will gather thee in all places whither thou goest, and will bring thee again into this land: for I will not leave thee, until I have done that which I have spoken to thee of." [1]

This was Jacob's dream. It was a rather odd dream considering the circumstances and the time from whence it came. To an unenlightened reader it might appear to be the hallucination of a road weary traveler seeking shelter from daytime fatigue. But, if you look carefully, you can perceive several interrelated promises enveloped into one vision. This vision was from God to Jacob. Jacob saw something. He sensed something and it terrified him. Let's explore this scenario further…

At the time of this dream, Jacob was running from his brother Esau. Esau was Jacob's older brother who was in line for the birthright inheritance from Isaac, their father. Esau, however, had already given up his birthright for a bowl of stew. Jacob had tricked Esau and now Jacob was in fear for his life. He ran! And then he dreamed.

This dream has come to be known as the stairway to heaven dream. Jacob saw a ladder ascending to the heavens and then he saw God standing above it. This, by itself, would be enough to frighten anybody. Then God spoke. He confirmed to Jacob that the birthright was intended for Jacob, all along, and for his descendants. God also made mention of the land upon which Jacob slept. He said: "the land whereon thou liest, to thee will I give it, and to thy seed." [2] Notice what is being stated here carefully. The land was to be an inheritance and so was the stone that Jacob slept on. Jacob took stones to be his pillow.

"And Jacob rose up early in the morning, and took the stone that he had put for his pillows, and set it up for a pillar, and poured oil upon the top of it. And he called the name of that place Bethel; but the name of that city was called Luz at the first. And Jacob vowed a vow, saying, If God will be with me, and will keep me in this way that I go, and will give me bread to eat, and raiment to put on so that I can come again to my father's house in peace: then shall the Lord be my God. And this STONE, which I have set for a pillar, shall be God's house: and of all that thou shalt give me I will surely give the tenth unto thee." [3]

First, we have a place called Bethel. [4] Bethel means house of God. This city is a place near Jerusalem that is still in existence today. It has a long Biblical history connected to it and just as long a Biblical promise connected to it. It is a city just north of Jerusalem, which is now in the area of the West Bank. This is one of the areas that the Palestinians are fighting so diligently to control. They want this landmass because it doesn't belong to them. Is this just a coincidence? God promised Jacob that "Jacob" would once again be regathered to this land. This promise is yet to be fulfilled. [5]

Second, we have an anointed stone with promise. If this is not strange in itself, it gets more uncanny. After anointing the stone with oil, Jacob gives the stone the title of God's house. So the stone is now the Bethel stone. Now we have a city named Bethel as well as a stone, which are soon to be separated. The further we delve into this historical drama, the more significant this will all become.

Third, Jacob makes a promise to God. He promises God that if God will take care of him and feed him, he will give ten percent of his descendant's back to God. This appears to be a first fruit offering. It is something to think about as we head into the millennium and the turn of the century. Where are the descendants of Jacob today? And where is Israel? Only a remnant will return.

Israel is the name that God gives to Jacob when he returns to Bethel a second time. Twenty-two years, and eleven sons later, Jacob becomes Israel. This name means Prince of God. It can also be construed to mean, sons ruling with God. God appears to Jacob once again and blesses him: "And God said unto him, Thy name is Jacob: thy name shall not be called any more Jacob, but Israel shall be thy name: and he called his name Israel. And God said unto him, I am God almighty: be fruitful and multiply; a nation and a company of nations shall be of thee' and kings shall come out of thy loins." [6]

Do you see a pattern here? First, Jacob is promised the land as well as a stone that is affiliated with that land. The city Bethel means house of God. The stone Bethel also means house of God. The stone becomes the pillar of Jacob, and goes forth with him from that day forward. These are the promised inheritances that God gives to Jacob and his descendants.[7]

Twenty-two years after this incident, God gives Jacob a name change. God appears to him again and renames him Israel, which means prince of God, and sons ruling with God. God, then, promises Israel a country and a group of countries. From all this, it appears that Israel is to become a migratory, ruling group.[8]

I must mention Joseph, the favorite son of Jacob. He was the eleventh son of Jacob by his loved wife Rachel who had been barren up until this birth. Joseph was a visionary child. He had inspired dreams and he retold these dreams to his brothers and to his father. One such dream was a dream that he was to rule over his brothers. His brothers hated him for it. In anger and betrayal they sold him and told Jacob, their father, that wild animals had killed him. Joseph went through a series of trials and imprisonment before he became a visionary interpreter of dreams. Because of his abilities, Pharaoh made him second man in Egypt. He was given high responsibility and authority. Eventually, Joseph's brothers came to him because of a famine in the land. Joseph, out of the greatness of his heart, forgave his brothers, and provided provisions for them. He made sure they were well taken care of and fed. Joseph was also reunited with his father, Jacob, before his death. Keeping this in mind, we arrive at the deathbed of Jacob; "Israel."

Jacob is near death when Joseph is called to him with his two children, Manasseh and Ephraim. Jacob speaks to Joseph of his encounter with God at Bethel. Then he takes Manasseh and Ephraim to his side to bless them. Manassah is the first born, but Joseph places his right hand on the head of Ephraim, which denotes the giving of the birthright to Ephraim instead of Manassah. This displeases Joseph who reminds his father that Manassah is the firstborn, and therefore in line for the first-born blessing. Joseph takes his father's right hand and places it on the head of Manassah. Then he takes his fathers left hand and puts it on the head of Ephraim. Jacob quickly objects and switches hands, then says. "I know it, my son. I know it; he also shall become a people, and he also shall be great: but truly his younger brother shall be greater than he, and his seed shall become a multitude of nations." [9] So, the birthright goes from Jacob to Joseph, and then to Ephraim.

Next, Jacob gathers his twelve sons together and proceeds to explain what will happen to them in the last days. This is futuristic prophecy. If we are now in the last days, as I believe we are, these prophecies pertain to this day and age. It is important to keep this in mind as you navigate the pages of this book.

"Rueben, thou art my firstborn, my might, and the beginning of my strength, the excellency of dignity, and the excellency of power: Unstable as water, thou shalt not excel; because thou wentest up to thy father's bed; then defiledst thou it: he went up to my couch." [10]

"Simeon and Levi are brethren; instruments of cruelty are in their habitations. O my soul, come not thou into their secret; unto their assembly, mine honour, be not thou united: for in their anger they slew a man, and in their self will they digged down a wall. Cursed be their anger, for it was fierce; and their wrath for it was cruel: I will divide them in Jacob, and scatter them in Israel." [11]

"Judah, thou art he whom thy brethren shall praise: thy hand shall be in thy neck of thy enemies; thy father's children shall bow down before thee. Judah is a lion's whelp: from thy prey, my son, thou art gone up: he stooped down, he couched as a lion, and as an old lion; who shall rouse him up? The sceptre shall not depart from Judah, nor a lawgiver from between his feet, until Shiloh come; and unto him shall the gathering of the people be."[12]

"Zebulun shall dwell at the haven of the sea; and he shall be for a haven of ships; and his border shall be unto Zidon." [13]

"Issachar is a strong ass couching down between two burdens: And he saw that rest was good, and the land that it was pleasant; and bowed his shoulder to bear, and became a servant unto tribute." [14]

"Dan shall judge his people, as one of the tribes of Israel. Dan shall be a serpent by the way, an adder in the path, that biteth the horse heels, so that his rider shall fall backward. I have waited for thy salvation, O Lord." [15]

"Gad, a troop shall overcome him: but he shall overcome at the last." [16]

"Out of Asher his bread shall be fat, and he shall yield royal dainties." [17]

"Naphtali is a hind let lose: he giveth goodly words." [18]

"Joseph is a fruitful bough, even a fruitful bough by a well; whose branches run over the wall. The archers have sorely grieved him, and shot at him, and hated him: But his bow abode in strength, and the arms of his hands were made strong by the hands of the mighty God of Jacob; (from thence is the shepherd, the stone of Israel:)." [19]

"Benjamin shall raven as a wolf: In the morning he shall devour the prey, and at night he shall divide the spoil." [20]

These are the prophecies and the blessings that Jacob prophesied to his children before he died. The sceptre was given to Judah portraying the ruling authority and dominance of this tribe. The stone and the shepherd are to come out from Joseph. This is a strange prophecy, indeed. Where is the stone today and who, what, where, and why is the shepherd to come out of Joseph? The answers to these questions should become revelatory as the pages of this little book unfold.

Chapter Three

Bible Covenants and God's promise to David

Covenants are interwoven throughout the pages of the Bible. A covenant is a binding agreement between two or more participants. A covenant can be spoken or written. It can be conditional or unconditional. God made many covenants at different periods of time down throughout the historical pages of the Bible. These covenants actually shaped history and formed our world into what it is today. The importance of a covenant within the context of the Bible should never be underestimated or oversimplified because covenants are the key to understanding the entire Bible.[1]

The paramount goal of a covenant is to establish a bond relationship between God and man. God desired to develop and maintain a relationship with his human children, more so than his children desired to maintain one with him. These bond relationships were always strained and eventually modified due to the disobedience of human beings and their innate flawed character. Time and time again, God would alter and modify his covenants to make provisions for the failings of man. God would continually reach out to embrace his creation and envelop them with his love. Covenants were established with the well being of mankind in mind and they always passed from God to a chosen intermediary. These intermediaries were chosen heirs, prophets, or both that God saw as suitable recipients of his promise. Each chosen intermediary had specific character strength that God looked for in a leader and was chosen as God's mouthpiece and negotiator for his word- the covenant of that dispensation. [2] These covenants and the prophecies that go with them serve to correlate seemingly unrelated Biblical, historical events.

Covenants are necessary to establish order on earth. Since a covenant is a relationship between God and man, they began as reciprocal agreements that were usually conditional. The first Edenic covenant is an example of this. It was conditional upon Adam and Eve's obedience. They disobeyed and the whole earth was plunged into a cycle of sin and death. God saw the inability of man to be perfect so he began to establish covenants with certain recipients that were unconditional and based solely on God's trustworthiness and faithfulness. This is how covenants maintain order. If every covenant between God and man had remained conditional, the human species would have expired in the beginning of creation. God's covenants maintain order. Many people might argue this point claiming God does nothing about suffering, misery and injustice. Although they would be partially correct, God is bound to his covenants and while they do keep order, man has been given a long leash.

God made his covenants from where he sits. Although we may not see the big picture, rest assured that God does. His authority is omnipotent but he can not go against his unconditional covenants unless he has stated beforehand the stipulations that will allow him to do so. Every promise that is written in the pages of the Bible, that is declared through God, or a prophet of God, will be fulfilled. You must understand that in order for God to fulfill every blessing and every curse, he has had to do a lot of manipulating and maneuvering down throughout history. All this takes time. God will fulfill all when everything is in its proper and strategic position. It may not be to human expectation but everything written will be accomplished.

It is too simplistic to separate the Bible into two basic and convenient covenants. Although, technically, the Bible can be divided into the Law covenant of Moses, and the Grace covenant of Jesus through the gospel of Paul, there is more to it than this. [3] While it is true that Jesus came and died for our sins, making intercession for mans' failure to keep the law of Moses there are more than two Bible covenants overlapping the pages of the Bible. The covenant given to Moses for the salvation of Israel was too arduous for the majority of the Israelites to keep, therefore God sent his son, Jesus, to die for our sins so we could seek his perfection and live eternally with God. A time is rapidly approaching when previous covenants will be reinstated to finish the declarations of all that God's prophets have declared down through the pages of the Bible. Hard and fast decisions will have to be made by the majority of mankind. We've had it too plentiful and too good for too long. Let's take a look at the reasons Jesus came.

When Jesus appeared on the scene, he claimed to be the Son of God, as well as the son of David. (This is beginning to sound an awful lot like the Davidic covenant).[4] He went to the Jews claiming that he was the Christ, which, by the way, means anointed. The Davidic kingdom was in need of restoration and unification. Jesus was sent forth to seek the Jews and the lost sheep of Israel. [5]

"And Jesus went about all the cities and villages, teaching in their synagogues, and preaching the gospel of the kingdom, and healing every sickness and every disease among the people." [6]

Jesus was searching for those who, by birth, were entitled to become a part of the Kingdom. Here is another example…

"Now after that John was put in prison, Jesus came into Galilee, preaching the gospel of the Kingdom of God, saying, the time is fulfilled, and the Kingdom of God is at hand; repent ye and believe the gospel." [7]

Jesus was a man, as well as the Son of God, who claimed his inherited birthright as the Messiah of all Israel. He was misunderstood, rejected, and then killed without completing his destiny. All that he was trying to do was to restore the Kingdom of David to legitimate subjects. Why was Jesus unable to fulfill his claim and purpose here on earth? [8] It has to do with prophecy that will unravel itself as history progresses.

The Bible begins in the Garden of Eden with Gods' creations, Adam and Eve. Adam and Eve are given responsibility to care for and tend the animals and the garden. Their lives were simple and God gave them everything they needed to be happy. One restriction was placed on them. They were not to eat of the tree of the knowledge of good and evil. God told them that if they did eat of this tree, they would die.

Well, as you might guess, the serpent tempted eve. Eve was very naive. Even though God had explained to her that she would die if she ate a certain fruit, the serpent was very cunning. He explained to Eve that she would not die if she ate the fruit, but would, instead, gain wisdom and insight. Eve ate the fruit and convinced Adam to do the same. This began the curse of creation. Man disobeyed and suffered the consequences, which included hard labor, childbirth, and death. This is the first covenant God made with man.

The Noahic covenant is another covenant made with humans. [9]This one is unconditional, made between God and Noah, and his sons, after the flood. It introduced human government to protect the sanctity of human life. Capital punishment was also introduced as a consequence of breaking that sanctity. Man is granted permission to eat the flesh of animals, which is newly introduced in this covenant. After the great God promised Noah that he would never again destroy the earth with a deluge. The rainbow is Gods' manifestation of that promise as a perpetual reminder of this covenant.

The next major covenant is made between God and Abraham.[10] This unconditional covenant was actually the beginning of a long, descending bond between God, a certain man, and then between God and certain of this man's descendants. The Abrahamic covenant marked an extremely important beginning of a "new" covenant between God and man.

God chose Abraham as the patriarch of his chosen nation. The nation status is the first part of this covenant to Abraham. And God said to Abraham..."And I will make of thee a great nation, and I will bless thee, and make thy name great; and thou shalt be a blessing: And I will bless them that bless thee, and curse them that curseth thee: and in thee shall all the families of the earth be blessed." [11]

The second part of this covenant from God to Abraham guaranteed land to the descendants of Abraham. This is sometimes called the "Palestinian Covenant." It was a promise that God would regather scattered Israel and bring them back to Jerusalem and the surrounding areas. This covenant was reaffirmed with Jacob at Bethel.

Moses was God's chosen leader to the children of Israel. God gave Moses the Ten Commandments along with other statutes to be followed. This was a conditional covenant that was dependent on obedience. It condemns all men...

"And Moses went up unto God and the Lord called unto him out of the mountain, saying, Thus shalt thou say to the house of Jacob, and tell the children of Israel; Ye have seen what I did unto the Egyptians, and how I bare you on eagles wings, and brought you unto myself. Now therefore, if you will obey my voice indeed, and keep my covenant, then you shall be a peculiar treasure unto me above all people: for all the earth is mine:" [12]

This old covenant was imperfect so a new one was needed. Jesus came to die for the sins of the world so that they could be partakers of the new, everlasting, unconditional covenant that is to impart a renewed mind and heart to the recipients. Some say this covenant was fulfilled in Jesus. I say it is only partially fulfilled at this time but will be complete at the Second Coming of Jesus. The reason that I say that it is only partially fulfilled at this time is that restored blessing and favor for Israel has not yet been fulfilled. Complete and final forgiveness of sin and the removal of all sin have not yet occurred. While Jesus died for our sins, we still succumb to sin. Here are the conditions of the terms of this new covenant.

"Behold, the days come, saith the Lord, that I will make a new covenant with the house of Israel, and with the house of Judah: Not according to the covenant that I made with her fathers in the day that I took them by the hand to bring them out of the land of Egypt; which my covenant they brake, although I was an husband unto them saith the Lord: But this shall be the covenant that I will make with the house of Israel: After those days, saith the Lord, I will put my law in their inward parts, and write it in their hearts; and will be their God, and they shall be my people." [13]

The final fulfillment of this unconditional covenant is still to be realized. This will entail the actualization of all the prophesied promises reaching their climactic conclusion. [14]

David was chosen and anointed by Samuel, the prophet, years before his actual reign began. He ruled from 1006-966 BC. First, he ruled in Hebron for seven years. Then he unified the Kingdom, which included all the tribes of Israel, and sought a new capital. He chose Jerusalem, which is now called the City of David. From Jerusalem, David ruled an extensive empire and he laid the groundwork for the building of Solomon's temple. God restricted him from actually building the temple because he was a warrior guilty of shedding blood. David was the greatest King Israel ever saw and was deeply loved by God. The qualifications that made him a great King included…his love of God, his ability to strategize as a warrior, his organizational skills, and his compassion. There are more. Although he sinned, he was forgiven. And God made a great covenential promise to David. This promise is given in the book of Samuel.

"Now therefore so shalt thou say unto my servant David, Thus saith the Lord of hosts, I took thee from following the sheep, to be ruler over my people, over Israel: And I was with thee whithersoever thou wentest, and have cut off all thine enemies out of thy sight, and have made thee a great name, like unto the name of the great men that are in the earth. Moreover I will appoint a place for my people Israel, and will plant them, that they may dwell in a place of their own, and move no more, neither shall the children of wickedness afflict them any more, as beforetime. And as such the time that I commanded Judges to be over my people Israel, and have caused thee to rest from all thine enemies. Also the Lord telleth thee that he will make thee an house. And when thy days be fulfilled, and thou shalt sleep with thy fathers, I will set up thy seed after thee, which shall proceed out of thy bowels, and I will establish his Kingdom. He shall build an house for my name, and I will establish the throne of his Kingdom forever." [15]

This was the covenant given to David from God. The first part of this promise says that Israel will be established as its' own country. Remember that Israel has been a migratory group down throughout history. So, somewhere at sometime, Israel was to have its' own country. This did not happen in the time of David because the United Kingdom of David divided in 926 BC, 44 years after David died. Apparently, Solomon, son of David, did not provide the type of leadership that was satisfactory to both houses, Judah and Israel. The next part of this promise guarantees that God will build a house for David. Specifically, God tells David, "I will make thee an house." The wordage used in the Authorized King James Version of the Bible is sometimes obscure. Some verses can be interpreted several ways. I believe this version of the Bible is the inspired word of God, so this is the version I will use throughout this book.

David is informed that after he dies, God will take of his descendents and establish his kingdom. A descendant of David will build a house to glorify God, and the throne of David will be made sure forever. Some theologians argue that since Solomon was the next reigning King from the lineage of David who built a glorious temple, then all succeeding Kings will come from his line. Some say that Jesus was of this line and he fulfilled this promise with his coming, death, and resurrection, and is now seated on this throne in heaven. But the promise says the throne will be made sure forever, so are either of these theories conclusively the right ones? Where is the throne of David located today? [16] And who sits on it? Let's conclude this chapter with II Samuel 7:13-16.

"He shall build an house for my name, and I will establish the throne of his Kingdom forever. I will be his father, and he shall be my son. If he commit iniquity, I will chasten him with the rod of men, and with the stripes of the children of men: But my mercy shall not depart away from him, as I took it from Saul, whom I put away before thee. And thine house and thine kingdom shall be established forever before thee: thy throne shall be established forever." [17]

Chapter Four

Solomon's Rise and Fall

In the last chapter, I showed how God made an unconditional, everlasting covenant with David. This covenant is guaranteed. It can not be annulled. It can not be broken. It promised David that a never-ending kingdom and throne would be established through his lineage. Think about this for a moment. Let's begin by taking a look at the children of David, beginning in II Samuel 3…

"And unto David were sons born in Hebron: and his firstborn was Amnon, of Ahinoam the Jezreelitess, and his second, Chileab, of Abigail the wife of Nabal the Carmelite; and the third, Absalom the son of Maacah the daughter of Talmai king of Geshur; And the fourth, Adonijah the son of Haggith; and the fifth, Shephatiah the son of Abitail, and the sixth, Ithream, by Eglah David's wife. These were born to David in Hebron" [1]

Then David went to Jerusalem and had more children. "And these be the names of those that were born unto him in Jerusalem; Shamua, and Shobab, and Nathan, and Solomon, Ibhar also, and Elishua, and Nepheg, and Japhia, and Elishama, and Eliada and Eliphalet." [2]

David fathered many children but Nathan stands out among his descendants.[3] Nathan is the prophet who condemned David for adultery. He is the prophet that announces to David that the "house" of

David would be made certain through the power of God. Nathan is the same prophet who works behind the scenes to establish Solomon as king, and then he is given authorization to anoint Solomon. Let's review...

"Then the king said unto Nathan the prophet, See now, I dwell in an house of cedar, but the ark of God dwelleth within curtains. And Nathan said to the king, Go, do all that is in thine heart: for the Lord is with thee. And it came to pass that night, that the word of the Lord came unto Nathan, saying, Go and tell my servant David, Thus saith the Lord, Shalt thou build me an house for me to dwell in? Whereas I have not dwelt in any house since the time that I brought up the children of Israel out of Egypt, even to this day, but have walked in a tent and in a tabernacle." [4]

"And as since the time that I commanded Judges to be over my people Israel, and have caused thee to rest from all thine enemies. Also the LORD telleth thee that he will build thee an house." [5]

Nathan also boldly denounces David for his adultery with Bathsheba. He tells David that his sin of killing Uriah, the husband to Bathsheba, is forgiven, but their child will die. David prays and fasts that the child may live, but it is to no avail. The child dies. Although Nathan denounces David for the sins of adultery and murder, he promotes the coronation of Solomon on the throne of David. Solomon is a son that is also born between the union of David and Bathsheba. Nathan is determined that Solomon will rule.

"Wherefore Nathan spoke unto Bathsheba the mother of Solomon, saying, hast thou not heard that Adonijah the son of Haggith doth reign, and David our Lord knoweth it not? Now therefore come, let me, I pray thee, give thee counsel, that thou mayest save thine own life, and the life of thy son Solomon, Go and get thee in unto King David, and say unto him, Didst not thou, my lord, O King, swear unto thine handmaid, saying, Assuredly Solomon thy son shall reign after me, and he shall sit upon my throne? Why then doth Adonijah reign?" [6]

David confirms that Solomon will indeed sit upon the throne of David and rule.

"And king David said, Call me Zadok the priest, and Nathan the prophet, and Benaiah the son of Jehoiada. And they came before the King. The king also said unto them, Take with you the servants of your lord, and cause Solomon my son to ride upon my own mule, and bring him down to Gihon: And let Zadok the priest and Nathan the prophet anoint him there King over Israel: And blow ye with the trumpet, and say, God save King Solomon. Then ye shall come up after him, that he may come and sit upon my throne; for he shall be King in my stead: and I have appointed him to be ruler over Israel and over Judah." [7]

Nathan the prophet has significance to the last of the last days as well, particularly in affiliation with the perpetual dynasty of David. Keep in mind that Nathan is the name of one of David's sons. There is a correlation here that will become self evident before the conclusion of this book. Now let us take a look at the blessing and promise passed on through David to Solomon.

David summoned Solomon to his side prior to his demise. David delegated to his son, Solomon, solemn responsibility to walk in the way of the Lord, to keep his statutes, judgements and commandments and to remain loyal to the Law of Moses. If Solomon stayed true to these statutes, then he would prosper in all of his endeavors. There seems to be a conditional clause placed upon Solomon and the retaining of the promise. David advised Solomon to follow the statutes.

"That the Lord may continue his word which he spake concerning me, saying, If thy children take heed to their way, to walk before me in truth with all their heart and all their soul, there shall not fail thee (said he) a man on the throne of Israel." [8]

David also gave Solomon the responsibility for building a house for God, since; God denied that charge to David. David prepared all the materials and labor to accomplish this monumental task. David explained to Solomon that God spoke to him regarding the building of a temple that would be built by Solomon. He also explained that a royal throne would be established forever.[9]

Let's review the conditions of the covenants between God and David, between David, Nathan, and Solomon, and then between David and Solomon. First, God makes an unconditional promise to David to give Israel a land to call its' own. Then, God promises to make a "house" out of David. Next, he assures David that of his lineage (he is not told specifically which line) a perpetual kingdom and throne will be established forever. Second, Nathan the prophet, Zadok the priest, and Benaiah the son of Jehoiada are instructed by David to anoint Solomon King over Israel. Then, they are instructed to come up after him so that Solomon may sit on the throne of David in his place. "And I have appointed him to be ruler over Israel and over Judah." [10] Third, David assures Solomon, that if he keeps the laws of God, there would not fail to be a man, from his lineage, to rule on the throne of Israel. Fourth, a promise comes to David from God…

"Behold, a son shall be born to thee, who shall be a man of rest; and I will give him rest from all his enemies round about: for his name shall be Solomon, and I will give peace and quietness unto Israel in his days. He shall build an house for my name; and he shall be my son, and I will be his father; and I will establish the throne of his Kingdom over Israel forever." [11]

And Solomon built God a beautiful temple. This building was a most splendid and glorious monument dedicated to the God of Israel. It was a reflection of the divine favor God had promised to David through Solomon. This temple was overlaid with gold and precious gems and the splendor was not to be compared with any other. Solomon covered the inner part (where the Ark of the Covenant went) of the temple with gold and gold was strewn across the front of the inner part of the sanctuary, and then he covered that with gold. The entire temple was embellished with gold and gold covered the entire house from start to finish. In the sanctuary, Solomon made two cherubim out of wood. He placed a cherubim in the inner part of the temple and the wings of this cherubim were stretched out so that each wing touched an adjoining wall. And the cherubim were also covered with gold. This was a magnificent temple.

After this temple was complete, in the year 953 BC, Solomon dedicated this effort to the Lord God of Israel. A grand festival was conducted and Solomon gave an elaborate oration. Prayers of dedication and thanksgiving were given to God. An enormous offering of 22,000 oxen and 120,000 sheep were sacrificed. A feast for all the children of Israel followed. It was a glorious occasion.[12] The Lord appeared to Solomon after this dedication.

"And the Lord said unto him, I have heard thy prayer and thy supplication, that thou has made before me: I have hallowed this house, which thou hast built, to put my name there forever; and mine eyes and mine heart shall be there perpetually. And if thou wilt walk before me, as David thy father walked, in integrity of heart, and in uprightness, to do according to all that I have commanded thee, and wilt keep my statutes and my judgements: Then I will establish the throne of thy kingdom upon Israel forever, as I promised to David thy father, saying, There shall not fail thee a man upon the throne of Israel." [13]

This promise to Solomon was conditional. Solomon departed from the ways of God. He took 700 wives and 300 concubines. He formed many allegiances with foreign countries and he allowed idolatry to enter into his kingdom. The maintenance of the splendor of the temple created a situation where high taxes and forced labor were called for. This eventually resulted in civil disobedience, and the division of the ten northern tribes of Israel from the southern division (Judah and Benjamin).

All of these conflicting promises are confusing. First, the promise to David is unconditional and everlasting. An heir is promised through his lineage that will establish this kingdom. A house and a throne of David are to be a continual certainty. Second, God promises David that

Solomon will indeed build a house for God, and the throne of his Kingdom will be made certain and perpetual over Israel. This is guaranteed! Third, God affirms a covenant to Solomon with conditions placed upon it.

"But if ye shall at all turn from following me, ye or your children, and will not keep my commandments and my statutes which I have set before you, but go and serve other gods and worship them: Then will I cut off Israel out of the land which I have given them; and this house which I have hallowed for my name, will I cast out of my sight; and Israel shall be a proverb and a byword among all people." [14]

The last part of the agreement is conditional which is evident by the contradictions going on here. We know the covenant with David is secure and perpetual. The covenant with David regarding Solomon is guaranteed. But, then this same reinstated covenant between God and Solomon is made conditional. How can this be?

From the context of this writing, let me try to explain these inconsistencies. An unconditional covenant is made to David. This covenant has absolutely nothing to do with obedience. It has at least a two-fold application. First, it has a corporeal application. Land is promised to Israel in this agreement. It also promises that God will make a "house" out of David. We will explore later where that house might be. Then, God promises David that a kingdom and a throne will be established through the lineage of David, on earth, forever. Second, this application includes a corporeal alongside a spiritual Kingdom. This spiritual kingdom will be the millennial rule on earth with Jesus as the chief ruler. This kingdom will also arrive through the lineage of David. A certain number of the twelve tribes of Israel are sealed to go into this kingdom in physical bodies. A certain chosen group "the elect" will be the rulers, priests, and authorities in this kingdom. [15] They will be in resurrected bodies. These chosen ones will be of the lineage of David through a certain combination of Israelite descent.

The promises to Solomon have a two-fold application. The first promise is unconditional. God promises David that Solomon will indeed build a house for the Lord, God, and the throne of Solomon's kingdom will be established over Israel forever.[16] This promise is futuristic. It pertains to the construction of the next temple in Jerusalem, with a descendant of Solomon who will be instrumental in building it. This same descendant will be the governor over Judah and Israel in the millennial kingdom to come. The second promise is conditional. God speaks to Solomon and is informed that if he turns from following the Laws and statutes of God, Israel will be cut off (at this time Israel is all twelve tribes in Jerusalem and surrounding areas.) and the house that Solomon built will be destroyed. God tells Solomon that Israel will become a proverb and a byword.[17]

Israel indeed became a byword and a proverb among all the people of the world. Most people do not know who, or where Israel is. Some think that only the Jews comprise Israel. [18] Others do not know what became of the lost tribes of Israel; some think they all died out. All that most people can agree upon is that Israel is lost to history and is no longer relevant to the understanding of the Bible since the gospel of grace came to be.

Chapter Five

A Divided Kingdom and The Fallen Temple

Before I begin to expound on where the tribes of Israel went and settled, I will first begin an attempt to satisfactorily explain the fallen temple of Solomon, and what became of the kingdom. After the death of Solomon, Rehoboam, son of Solomon, took over as the newly anointed king. He chose Shechem as the place for his capital rather than Jerusalem. The reason for this is unclear, but it appears that the northern kingdom of Israel came to Shechem to anoint Rehoboam king there. At this time the kingdoms of Israel and Judah were newly divided, and Rehoboam was the appointed ruler over the southern kingdom (Judah and Benjamin) but not over the rest of Israel.[1]

Rehoboam was approached by Jeroboam, the newly appointed king of the northern kingdom. Jeroboam desired to reunite the two houses of Israel under certain specifications that could be agreed upon by both kingdoms. Jeroboam, an Ephratite, was eager to serve Rehoboam; and all of Israel was there to support this move on Jeroboams' behalf. The only stipulation required by the Israelites was that Rehoboam lighten the burdensome taxes, and perhaps rules, that had been imposed on them by the former King Solomon.

King Rehoboam consulted with the older dignitaries who had been servants to Solomon. These older men advised Rehoboam to become a servant to the people of Israel and listen to their needs. If he did this, Israel would remain a loyal servant to him and the kingdom would once again be reunited. Instead, King Rehoboam departed from the wisdom of the elders and took up counsel with the younger men who had grown up with Rehoboam. These younger men advised Rehoboam to increase the oppression upon Israel, and subject them to added taxation. The northern kingdom of Israel abruptly departed. This was God's will.

The ten northern tribes kept Jeroboam as their King. The southern kingdom, which was comprised of Judah, as well as Benjamin, was left under the jurisdiction of Rehoboam. While Jerusalem was once again the religious capital of Judah, the northern kingdom had no place to worship. Bethel and Dan, cities of the territory of Jeroboam, were designated as worship centers for the ten northern tribes. Jeroboam immediately made a golden calf, which represented pagan idolatry. This marked the beginning of the decline of the northern kingdom as well as the subsequent loss of leadership in Israel.

After the death of Jeroboam, Nadab became King of Israel. Baasha slays him and rules instead. Baasha dies and Elah, his son, rules instead. Zimri kills Elah and rules as King of Israel next. Zimri commits suicide by burning the King's house while he is in it. After him, Israel is divided into two kingdoms. Half of Israel follows Tibni, and half of Israel follows Omri. Omri is a stronger King. Tibni dies and Omri rules over reunited Israel. Ahab rules after the death of his father, Omri. The list goes on. All of the Kings over Israel did wickedly in the eyes of God. Eventually, Israel is exiled into Assyrian captivity.

Rehoboam, son of Solomon, which then passes to Abijam, rules the southern Kingdom. After the death of Abijam, Asa, his son, reigns in his place. Asa does what is righteous in the eyes of God. Jehosophat, his son, rules after his death. He does not follow God's law. Jehoram, the son of Jehosophat, rules next. He does evil. After him, Ahaziah is King of Judah. He does wickedly and rules for only one year. Athaliah rules next. Then, Jehoash rules Judah. He does well during the time of his reign. The point is…Judah has more law-abiding kings than Israel. One King of special notation is Hezekiah.

Hezekiah is a righteous King during his reign over Judah. He is twenty-five years old when he begins to rule. His reign lasts twenty-five years in Jerusalem. Like David, his predecessor, he follows the laws of God and prospers as King. Hezekiah destroys the golden idols and does away with the high places. He drives the Philistines away from all the borders of the fenced cities that belong to Judah. During his reign, the Assyrians come up against Samaria and take away all Israel (ten northern tribes) into Assyria. Also, which many Bible scholars fail to mention, all of the fenced cities of Judah are also taken into Assyrian captivity several years after the ten northern tribes go into exile.[2]

This Assyrian captivity of the northern kingdom of Israel is a direct consequence of disobedience. The Kings of the northern tribes of Israel could not follow the rules of God. Because of this, the northern kingdom disintegrates to the point where self-rule is not in the best interest of the people. Once the strength of the Kingdom is gone, there are no strongholds. The Assyrians quickly take over.

The Assyrian captivity occurs during the reign of King Hezekiah. Even though Hezekiah is a devout leader, and lives in the fear of God, the fenced cities of Judah are all taken captive. Eight years after the siege of all Israel, an Assyrian King comes and takes all the fenced cities of Judah (excluding Jerusalem) into Assyrian exile. Hezekiah seeks God and stands his ground in regards to Jerusalem. Jerusalem is spared, for now. Sennacherib, King of Assyria, is destroyed.

God makes a prophetic promise to Hezekiah regarding Judah. "Hast thou not heard long ago how I have done it, and of ancient times that I have formed it? now have I brought it to pass, that thou shouldest be to lay waste fenced cities into ruinous heaps. Therefore their inhabitants were of small power, they were dismayed and confounded; they were as the grass of the field, and as the green herb, as the grass on the house-tops, and as corn blasted before it be grown up. But I know thy abode, and thy going out, and thy coming in, and thy rage against me. Because thy rage against me and thy tumult is come up into my ears, therefore I will put my hook in thy nose, and my bridle in thy lips, and I will turn thee back by the way by which thou camest. And this shall be a sign unto thee, Ye shall eat this year such things as grow of themselves, and in the second year that which springeth of the same; and in the third year sow ye, and reap, and plant vineyards, and eat the fruits thereof. And the remnant that is escaped of the house of Judah shall yet again take root downward and bear fruit upward. For out of Jerusalem shall go forth a remnant, and they that escape out of mount Zion: the zeal of the Lord of hosts shall do this. Therefore thus saith the Lord concerning the King of Assyria, He shall not come into this city, nor shoot an arrow there, nor come before it with shield, nor cast a bank against it." [3]

This appears to be futuristic prophecy as well as prophecy pertinent to the times of King Hezekiah. God tells Hezekiah that everything is in his power. In a nutshell he says, it is written; it is done. God is the supreme authority and he creates all things, for him, and through him. God informs Hezekiah that those of Judah that escape will again bear fruit. It appears that he is speaking about a remnant of Judah that will escape from their captors. A large percentage of Judah was taken into Assyrian captivity shortly after the ten tribes were taken. It appears that the house of Judah was also separated. Where did much of Judah end up? [4] It is becoming apparent that not only Israel lost their identity, but also so did a good proportion of Judah. Continuing, we find that God gives a specific prophecy concerning Jerusalem. He tells Hezekiah that a remnant will escape out of Jerusalem, only a remnant. This appears to pertain to the resulting Babylonian captivity of the inhabitants of Jerusalem.

The Babylonian captivity is a period in history that began in 597 BC.[5] A selective deportation took place first. The year was 597 BC, and the Babylonians forcefully took the "best" of Judah which included the upper class educated.[6] Next, a siege and war against Jerusalem took place in approximately the year 587 BC. The rest of Judah was taken to Babylon and the temple of Solomon was devastated and destroyed. This siege began the 70 year exile which ended in 516 BC. What final events led to this siege of Jerusalem? Let's examine the last Kings of Judah, beginning with Josiah.

King Josiah is the son of Manasseh (a very evil King) who is the son of Hezekiah. Josiah begins his rule at the tender age of eight. His leadership lasts thirty-one years. He is a just King who seeks to do what is right in the eyes of God. During his reign, the book of the law of God is found and delivered to Josiah. Josiah makes a covenant by the "pillar" to follow God's statutes. He destroys idolatry from the Kingdom, as well as magic and astrology. He also destroys all the shrines Jehoiakim, his son, rules after him.

Jehoiakim ruled over Jerusalem for a period of eleven years. "Jehoiakim was twenty and five years old when he began to reign; and he reigned eleven years in Jerusalem. And his mother's name was Zebudah, the daughter of Pediah of Rumah. And he did that which was evil in the sight of the Lord, according to all that his Fathers had done. In his days Nebuchadnezzar King of Babylon came up, and Jehoiakim became his servant three years: then he turned and rebelled against him. And the Lord sent against him bands of the Chaldees, and bands of the Syrians, and bands of the Moabites, and bands of the children of Ammon, and sent them against Judah to destroy it, according to the word of the Lord, which he spake by his servants the prophets." [7]

Coniah reigns in Jerusalem, after the death of Jehoiakim. He does not follow the laws of God, either. Jeremiah, a prophet, utters a prediction with regards to Coniah (Jeconias). "O earth, earth, earth, hear the word of the Lord. Thus saith the Lord, write ye this man childless, a man that shall not prosper in his days: For no man of his seed shall prosper, sitting upon the throne of David, and ruling any more in Judah." [8] Coniah is carried off into Babylonian exile.

Zedekiah rules next. He is the brother of Coniah's father. Nebuchadnezzar appointed him King over Jerusalem for eleven years. After this period, his sons are all murdered. Zedekiah is taken to Babylon, placed in prison, and his eyes are gouged out. Solomon's temple is plundered and destroyed.

Disobedience and disregard for the laws of God were the root cause of all this accumulative disaster. The majority of the Kings of both the northern and southern kingdoms succumbed to the temptations of pride, power, greed, and self will. Had the Kings followed the lead of David, their Kingdoms would not have been destroyed. Because Israel and Judah rebelled against God, disaster fell. Time and time again prophets of God warned them, but they did not listen. The Kingdoms fell.

What became of the dynasty of David? First, the Kingdoms were divided. This was God's will. Then, the northern kingdom went into Assyrian captivity. A good proportion of Judah was taken into Assyrian captivity several years later. Next, what was left of Judah, as well as Jerusalem, was taken captive. Jerusalem was looted and destroyed. Coniah (the cursed King), the second to the last ruling King of Judah, was carried off to Babylon. A curse is placed on his lineage, stating no man of his lineage would ever sit and rule on the throne of David again in Judah. Then, Zedekiah (an uncle to Coniah) reigns in Jerusalem. All of his sons are killed and his eyes are put out. As far as I know, Zedekiah was the last ruling King of Judah, in Jerusalem, from this succession of Solomon's lineage.

If the promises to David are bonafide, how could God have allowed this to happen? Let's step back and review. God made an unconditional promise to David. Nathan, the prophet, communicated this oath to David.[9]

"Also the Lord telleth thee that he will make thee an house. And when thy days be fulfilled, and thou shalt sleep with thy fathers, I will set up thy seed after thee, which shall proceed out of thy bowels, and I will establish his Kingdom. He shall build an house for my name, and I will stablish the throne of his Kingdom Forever. I will be his father, and he shall be my son. If he commit iniquity, I will chasten him with the rod of men, and with the stripes of the children of men:"[10] "And thine house and thy Kingdom shall be established for ever before thee: thy throne shall be established for ever." [11]

God makes an unconditional promise to David through Nathan. Take a close look at this oath. It guarantees a throne, Kingdom, and house of David will be established forever.[12] It doesn't specifically mention Solomon. There are no conditions. Now I have one ponderous question. Where did the descendents of Nathan go?

Further on, God makes a conditional promise to Solomon. "But if ye shall at all turn from following me, ye or your children, and will not keep my commandments and my statutes which I have set before you, but go and serve other gods and worship them: Then will I cut off Israel out of the land which I have given them; and this house which I have hallowed for my name will I cast out of my sight; and Israel shall be a proverb and a byword among all people." [13]

Solomon failed. Most of his direct descendents failed. So the Kingdom fell and the temple was destroyed. But is this the end of the story? Let's take a look at I Chronicles 22.

"Behold, a son shall be born to thee, who shall be a man of rest; and I will give him rest from all his enemies round about: for his name shall be Solomon, and I will give peace and quietness unto Israel in his days. He shall build an house for my name; and he shall be my son' and I will be his father; and I will establish the throne of his Kingdom over Israel for ever." [14] This promise is unconditional. There is more going on here than meets the eye. God can not lie and the Bible is not false. So, the questions that need to be asked are…Where is the house and kingdom of David today? Who are the descendents of Nathan? Where is Israel? [15] Who sits on the throne of Solomon? Who rules over Israel? These questions and their solutions will be explored as we search for the lost tribes of the collapsed Kingdoms.

Chapter Six

A Little History of The Invasions

The kingdoms of Judah and Israel divided after the reign of Solomon. This happened in approximately 927 BC. The Kingdom of Israel included the ten tribes of Israel, excluding the tribes of Judah and Benjamin. The Kingdom of Judah was comprised of the two tribes of Judah and Benjamin. It should be mentioned that part of Levi also went with Judah. These divided Kingdoms went their own ways, had separate Kings, and had their own judicial systems. At about 721 BC, the Kingdom of Israel was taken into Assyrian captivity. At, or about, 586 BC, the Kingdom of Judah was taken into Babylonian exile. For the sake of expediency, I will begin an overview of these invasions, beginning with the Babylonian exile. The reasons for this are: the migrations of the house of Judah are better documented and easier to follow than are the migrations of the house of Israel, and the main focus of this book deals with the lost tribes of Israel as far as the subject of the two witnesses is concerned. For these reasons, I have taken the invasions out of chronological order.

Babylon began to exile Judah, from their homeland, Jerusalem, in the approximate year 597 BC. This is only the beginning of the deportations. In the year 587 BC, Judah loses all independence. They become a "house" without a home, without a state, and without a nation. This is the period that has come to be known as the "exile" in Biblical history. With this loss of nation, it appears that the succession of the Davidic dynasty also comes to an end. The house of Judah is placed under the rulership of King Nebuchadnezzar of Babylon.[1]

This Babylonian exile lasts approximately 70 years. The deported Jews form their own community in Babylon, while clinging to their cherished religion and traditions. The majority of the house of Judah continued to worship the God of Abrahamn, Isaac, and Jacob. While most stayed true to their roots, some assimilated into the Babylonian culture, which included intermarriages and pagan religions.

After approximately 50-70 years, in the year 538 BC, the Jews are allowed to return to Jerusalem. The dates vary from source to source because the Babylonian exile actually took place in stages. What brought about the release of the Jewish exiles was the takeover of Babylon by the Persian Empire- under the leadership of Cyrus the Great in the year 539 BC. The following year, Cyrus grants the Jews freedom to return to Jerusalem.

The Jews are allowed to return home for religious purposes. Cyrus was a conquering ruler who believed in a dualistic universe between good and evil forces. He believed that the God of the Hebrews was a good force. Supposedly, Cyrus had a vision from the God of Jacob that motioned him to release the house of Judah, and allow them to return to Jerusalem to worship and to rebuild their temple. The temple was rebuilt and Judah was sent home. Some, but not all, of the people returned to Jerusalem to begin again.

For about 200 years, the Persian Empire controlled Egypt and all of the Middle East. This was a powerful group of people who believed in many gods, and the power of these gods. During this timespan, Palestine was subject to Persia. The Persian Empire was the dominant world power, and the house of Judah was allowed to worship their God. They did not have the power or the freedom that they once possessed.

This Persian control of Jerusalem continued until 332 BC when Jerusalem became a Greek State.

In the year 332 BC, Alexander the Great conquered the Persian Empire and usurped power. Along with the overthrown Empire came Jerusalem and Judah. After two centuries of being subject to Persian dominion, Judah finds itself thrust under subjection to a new power. Alexander the Great conquered Persia, and was now the controller of Jerusalem, as well as most of the rest of the world. After the death of Alexander the Great, power struggles ensued within the Greek Empire. Jerusalem was placed under seven different rulers between 319 and 302 BC.

During the Greek era, known as the Hellenistic period, many changes took place. The Greeks introduced a new concept called naturalization. Now a person could become a citizen of another state or country without being born there. Because of this, many from Judah chose to live in other places rather than their homeland of Jerusalem. Also, during the Hellenistic period, the Hebrew Bible was translated into Greek. The Torah, as the Jews call it, became the book of life to the Jews. The Greek intention in translating the Bible was to obtain copies to put into their libraries. This Greek translation of the Bible became known as the Septuagint, which means seventy. Is it only a coincidence that the Judaen exile lasted about 70 years?

Romans bring an end to the Jewish state in 70 AD.[2] This historical period is called the Diaspora, which means dispersion. The Romans forcefully take over and force the Jews from their homeland. During the Diaspora, Jerusalem is controlled by the Romans from 63 BC through 313. From 313 through 636, the Byzantine Empire rules Jerusalem. The Arabs control the area from 636 through 1099. Then, from 1099 through 1291 Jerusalem is under Latin control. From 1291 through 1516, the Mamluk rule. From 1517 through 1917, Jerusalem is under Ottoman rule.

The British take charge from 1918 through 1948. It is not until the British come to power that the Diaspora comes to an end. The homecoming has begun.[3]

Although, chronologically, the Assyrian captivity began many years earlier than the Babylonian captivity; the Assyrian captivity has been a huge mystery to history. It is only recently that documentation has been established of archaeological evidence that supports the migrations of the "ten lost tribes of Israel." Israel was lost only because God intended it to remain that way until the end of the age when he calls his people home.

The Assyrian captivity actually begins before the year 721 BC. [4] This is because the invasions of Israel took place in successive stages. The first stage began in approximately 741 BC. An account of the first invasion is mentioned in II Kings. At this time, Menahem was King over Israel.

" And Pul the King of Assyria came against the land: and Menahem gave Pul a thousand talents of silver, that his hand might be with him to confirm the Kingdom in his hand. And Menahem exacted the money of Israel, even of all the mighty men of wealth, of each man fifty shekels of silver, to give to the King of Assyria. So the King of Assyria turned back, and stayed not there in the land." [5]

From this account, it is clear that the first invasion was light. It is not really considered an invasion by all accounts because no captives were taken. It is clear that this invasion marks the beginning of the end for the house of Israel as far as self-rule is concerned.

The second invasion of Israel followed soon afterward. "In the days of Pekah King of Israel came Tiglath-Pileser King of Assyria, and took Ijon, and Abel beth-maacah, and Janoah, and Kedesh, and Hazor, and Giliad, and Galilee, all the land of Naphtali, and carried them captive to Assyria." [6] The second invasion was more severe. The cause of this invasion was a direct result of a conspiracy on the part of Pekah, King of

Israel, to attack and overthrow Judah. God was not pleased with this scheme.

According to E. Raymond Capt, archaeologist, historian, and author of Missing Links Discovered in Assyrian Tablets, more information is recorded in the annals of Tiglath-Pileser III. Here we discover that the tribes of Asher, Issachar, and Zebulun, were also deported and placed on the borders of Assyria, where cities were built. These cities were given names such as Sakka, Danium, Elisansa, Abrania, etc. and are traced to Israelite origins.[7]

The third invasion began in the approximate year 723 BC. and lasted until 721 BC. It was the most disastrous of all. Most of the Kingdom of Israel was taken to Assyria during this exile. The cause of this invasion was due to the King of Israel, Hoshea, who refused to pay Shalmanesar tribute. Also Hoshea requested assistance from the Egyptians, which was a threat to the Assyrian ambition.

Shalmanesar was King of Assyria at the beginning of the third invasion. Shalmanesar V, assumed the throne after the death of his father, Tiglath-Pileser in 725 BC. His reign was short. Shalmanesar V was credited with capturing Samaria and deporting the Israelites to Assyria. This may not be the complete, factual case. The successor to the throne of Shalmanesar, Sargon II, claims that he is the one who took at least 27,000 persons to Assyria. It appears from existing evidence that Shalmanesar died before the Assyrian captivity and deportation of the majority of the Israelites from the third invasion was complete. [8]

The third invasion can be summarized in II Kings. "Therefore the Lord was very angry with Israel, and removed them out of his sight: there was none left but the tribe of Judah only. Also Judah kept not the commandments of the Lord their God, but walked in the statutes of Israel which they made. And the Lord rejected all the seed of Israel, and afflicted them, and delivered them into the hand of the spoilers, until he had cast them out of his sight." [9]

This statement "cast them out of his sight" has Biblical significance. The people of God became castaways. They were no longer to find special favor from God because they were removed from the land portion of the house of God. (Bethel-area) "A Land which the Lord careth for: the eyes of the Lord thy God are always upon it, from the beginning of the year even unto the end of the year." [10]

In approximately the year 705 BC, while Hezekiah was the King of Judah, Sennachereb; reigning king of Assyria, came into the Judean territory. First, Sennacherib began to plunder and destroy cities outside Jerusalem. He took 46 fenced cities and removed about 200,000 captives from the tribe of Judah and planted them with the rest of the captive Israelites. The exploits of King Sennacherib are recorded in the "Taylor Prism," which can be found at the British Museum. These inscriptions contain evidence that is detailed by Sennacherib, himself, of his plunder and attacks upon the Judean Kingdom. [11]

The Bible gives us more information about the devastation of Sennacherib against Judah. "Now in the fourteenth year of King Hezekiah did Sennacherib King of Assyria come up against all the fenced cities of Judah and took them." [12] It should be noted that the city of Jerusalem was spared due to the righteousness and prayer of King Hezekiah.

What happened to the northern house of Israel, or Ephraim as it is sometimes called? [13] It is documented that a large percentage of Judah also went with them. Did they just disappear off the face of the earth? Did they all die off? Or did they travel together, lose their identities, and settle into areas adjacent to each other?

You will also soon discover that Israel never ceased to exist, but instead, thrived and became major players in world history. The tribes of Israel went on to fulfill their Biblical destinies, which includes all of the prophecies predicted by the prophets of God that involves them. Furthermore, the prophecies of the Bible are not yet complete. As I explain the purposes and the migrations of the descendants of

Abraham, Isaac, and Jacob, I intend to portray the Bible as a living history book that is yet to culminate in a glorious, climactic conclusion that ushers in the kingdom of God under Jesus. [14]

Chapter Seven

The Lost Israelites

Archaeological evidence has been found to substantiate where the tribes of Israel wandered. This evidence has come to light during the course of the past 150 years. Bits and pieces of archaeological confirmation have been unearthed of the records that the Assyrian captors kept themselves, that correlate with the historical period and the people that were of the house of Israel. These pieces have been put together to form pictures of the missing puzzle of Israel. These records today are kept in the British Museum.

Some of the more explicit evidence was found at Ninevah, in 1850 AD. This consists of pictures that Assyrian scribes engraved on clay, cuneiform tablets that record the Israelite migrations. These were translated and published around 1930, but their connection to Israel had not been determined at that time. The reason for this is that the Israelites were called by a variety of names by their captors, and these connections have just recently been discovered.

In 1861, in Southwestern Turkey, an early Assyrian illustration depicting the Israelites was found. It shows the King of Assyria saluting the Assyrian gods. Both sides of this stone record give credence to the historical conquest of the Israelites. On this stone, the Assyrian King inscribes his victory, of 853 BC, over a group of twelve Kings at the battle of Karkar, on the Orontes river. The record shows engraved pictures of the thwarted army of King Ahab, who was the King of the Northern Kingdom of Israel at that time. This record refers to "Ahab, the Israelite." It is the last record of the Assyrians calling the Israelites by that name.

In, or around, 841 BC the Israelites are referred to as the "House of Omri". This term applies to the Kingdom of Israel and to Jehu, the successor of Ahab. At this time Jehu is put under the domination of Shalmaneser, King of Assyria. This is shown in Assyrian script where Jehu, King of Israel, is paying tribute to the Assyrian captors. The title Omri is shown to go slight variations of spelling and pronunciation. So, in some places, Omri is spelled Ghomri, and then Khumri. The last reference to the Khumri is made by Sargon II, who calls himself the conqueror of "Bit-Khumri." This was the ruler of Assyria from 722-705 BC. During this period, part of the Assyrian captivity takes place.[1]

According to evidence discovered, the Israelites, who were called "Khumri" at first by the Assyrians, were held captive in northern Assyria near a river called Habor, and also they were placed with the Medes in Iran. At this point, the Israelites became known as the Gimera and the Cimmerians. Even though these Cimmerians were in close proximity with the people of Medes, they remained a distinct people. While these Cimmerians accounted for a portion of the Israelites taken into exile, it does not account for all of them.

What became of the rest of the Israelites that were carried off into Assyrian captivity? According to E. Raymond Capt., archaeologist, historian, and author of Missing Links Discovered in Assyrian Tablets, there was a group of people called Iskuza that are mentioned in some discovered prayer texts of Esarhaddon to his son-god. Iskuza lived among the Mannai people. One such prayer text reads: "Will the Iskuza warriors who live in the district of the Mannai, succeed in their plan? Will they march out from the pass of Hubushkia and reach the towns of Harrania and Anisukia, and take much booty and heavy spoil from the borders of Assyria?" Other prayer texts demonstrate that the Iskuza raided Medes and competed with the Assyrians that were sent there to collect tribute.[2]

The Iskuza is believed to be an Assyrian name of another group of Israelites that originally migrated to Asia Minor, whereas the Cimmerians were the ones planted in Media. Iskuza appears to be a variation of Isaac. The Israelites were sometimes called the "House of Isaac" from Abrahamn, Isaac, and Jacob. It is universally accepted by modern historians that the Iskuza were called Shuthae by the Greeks and Sacae (also Saka and Sakka) by the Persians. Herodotus further tells us the Persians called the Sacae, "Scythians."

At this point we have two related groups of Israelites that diverge into two separate branches. These are the Cimmerians and the Scythians that have been believed to be the lost tribes of Israel without verifiable proof for many, many years. With the archaeological find of the clay, cuneiform tablets and certain other "letters" which were found at Ashurbanipals royal Library at Kijunjik, in 1847, by English archaeologist, Austin Henry Layard while he was an attaché to the British Embassy in Constantinople, we now have confirmed evidence.[3]

The Cimmerians and Scythians continued to migrate and wander until they eventually joined together. Biblical references show some of the wanderings of the tribes of Israel that support the evidence that the lost tribes of Israel did not disappear into oblivion. II Esdras is the first example. "Those are the ten tribes, which were carried away prisoners out of their own land in the time of Oseo the King, whom Salmnasar the King of Assyria led away captive, and he carried them over the waters, and so came they into another land. But they took this counsel among themselves, that they would leave the multitude of the heathen, and go forth into a further country where never mankind dwelt. That they might there keep their statutes, which they never kept in their own land. And they entered into Euphrates by the narrow passages of the river. For the most High then shewed signs for them, and held still the flood, til they were passed over. For through that country there was a great way to go, namely, of a year and a half: and that same region is called Arsareth."[4]

Another example can be found in the book of Tobit. "the book of the words of Tobit, son of Tobiel, the son of Ananiel, the son of Aduel, the son of Gabael, of the seed of Asael, of the tribe of Naphthali: Who in the time of Enemessan King of the Assyrians was led captive out of Thisbe, which is at the right hand of that city, which is called properly Naphthali in Galilee above Aser. I Tobit have walked all the days of my life in the way of truth and justice, and I did many almsdeeds to my brethren, and my nation who came with me to Nineve, into the land of the Assyrians."[5]

Thus far, I have provided some historical backing as well as scriptural support for the continuing existence of the lost tribes of Israel after the exile to Assyria.[6] Now, let us continue to seek the truth of this matter further with the already established names of the Cimmerians and the Scythians who are the self-same people of Israel.

The Cimmerians arrived in the areas west from the Black Sea before the Scythian branch of the Israelites arrived. These first Cimmerians diverged into two branches. The first branch of the Cimmerians, which constituted the greater majority of these people, migrated into France, as well as traveling further into the British Isles of Ireland, Wales, and up into Scotland. Another branch of the Cimmerians went northwest into Holland, Belgium, and into Jutland, which is in the vicinity of Denmark. Some of these same people went further north into Norway. Both branches of these people became known as Cimry, Gaul, and Celts. These should and will be considered the first settlers from the dispersed lost tribes of Israel that came to northwest and northern Europe.

According to Yair Davidy, world recognized authority in the field of lost Israelite identity, the Cimmerians had already taken over central Europe between 600-550 BC, and began the foundation of Celtic civilization. By 450 BC, the bulk of the Celtic power was in France and Belgium. From there it moved into the British Isles. This began to occur in stages between 500-400 BC. Ireland was the first stop for many of these newcomers. From Ireland these people migrated into Scotland, West England, and Wales.[7]

An identifying mark that should be mentioned in conjunction with these first Cimmerian settlers is found in the Bible in the book of Jeremiah "Is Ephraim my dear son? is he a pleasant child? for since I spake against him, I do earnestly remember him still: therefore my bowels are troubled for him: I will surely have mercy upon him saith the Lord. Set thee up waymarks, make thee high heaps: set thine heart toward the highway, even the way which thou wentest: turn again, O virgin of Israel, turn again to these thy cities."[8]

"The following verse (31:21) in Jeremiah may well be referring to Dolmens which are large stones set table fashion over others and often covered by large piles of rocks and stone. The dolmens and other related stone monuments form a connecting link between Israel, Britain, West France, and Scandinavia. More Dolmens (over 5000) have been found in Denmark than in any other country. On the other hand the oldest dolmens are believed to be those in Israel and more than 20,000 megalithic monuments of all types (including dolmens) have been found in the land of Israel"(Davidy).[9]

If these monuments are somehow connected to these earlier, Cimmerian settlers of northwest Europe, as I believe they are, a basis has been established to connect the peoples of Israel with evidence linked to the Bible. Foundational evidence will have also been made that links these monuments to "Ephraim." Ephraim will be discussed later on in this writing due to its relevance to Bible prophecy.

It appears that the Cimmerian branch that traveled into Holland, Belgium and into Jutland and Denmark arrived at a later date (between 525-300 BC.) than the French, Irish, Welsh, and Scottish divergence did. These people may have carried a large element of Judah along with them. Jut is a form of Judah. This being so, we might consider Nathan, the son of David, as the progenitor of a large number of these peoples descendants.

The Naphtalites are shown to have migrated to Scandinavia. Along with the tribe of Naphtali, the Goths, Jutes, and Danes also traveled. This places the Jutes in close proximity to the Scandinavians."[10]

Whatever the case, the Cimmerians arrived before the Scythians. Certain tribes of Judah accompanied them. We have already ascertained that a large number of Judah went into Assyrian captivity with the Israelites. Keep in mind that these Judaens were never called Jews and they were seldom called Judah. They simply assimilated into the other tribes and became an element of them. Certain tribes in particular formed alliances with these people of Judah. Since Judah was a ruling tribe, common sense should tell us that the more aggressive tribes such as Ephraim and Dan would have been the first to form close associations with Judah.

There is not always clear cut differentiation between some of the Cimmerians and some of the Scythians. This is because the Israelite migrations through Europe came in successive undulations. What is certain is that the majority of Cimmerians that came first took a route through France, then into the British Isles. The Cimmerians that arrived through Holland, Belgium, and into Jutland, arrived a bit later and may well be a part of the royal Scythians who settled throughout Scandinavia.

The Scythians may have been considered outcasts of the Cimmerians. These Scythian Israelites, who arrived quite a bit later, were a people called Saca after Isaac, the father of Jacob. Israelite identification of the Saca-Scythian ties them to the House of Isaac. This is inferred by their association with the Cadussi who belonged to the Naphtali tribe.[11]

About 175 BC. a large number of Cadussi were at the border of China. A succession of occurrences happened on the borders of Mongolia at this time. The war like Huns drove the Yueh-Chi out of

China. These Yueh-Chi drove the Saka out of another area- near the Ili river. In 100 BC, a Saka Kingdom was formed between Afghanistan and Kashmin. They continued to migrate.[12]

After around 100 BC, the Scythians became known by other names, such as Sarmatae and the Germani. From these people came the Anglo-Saxon people and the subsequent Anglo-Saxon invasions of Europe. As we shall see, most of these invasions occurred after the birth and death of Jesus, which figures predominantly into Biblical history. Let's take a look at some of the heraldic symbols of the tribes of Israel.

Heraldry has long been used throughout history for identification purposes. Coat of arms, family crests, and emblems denoting tribal association has served to trace the family lineage of many different people. These heraldic identification symbols have always been passed down from generation to generation within a family. An emblem of one family is seldom used by another family.[13]

Keeping this in mind, we will take a look at the heraldic symbols of the people of the British Isles and of North-West and Northern Europe who have all adopted, from ancient times, symbols that are representative of the Israelite tribes. A depiction of a man is given to Rueben. If you recall the blessing from Jacob to his twelve sons, Rueben was not blessed much. That was because of his moral weakness. Rueben is also represented by water because of his instability. Countries that have used these emblems include Denmark, Greece, Iceland, and Sweden. A sword is the emblem of Simeon and Levi. The sword appears in many places in Britain and Ireland. A castle is Simeon's other emblem. It appears in at least 50 places in the British Isles. It also appears in Scotland. A lion is the symbol of Judah. This symbol appears in many royal and national arms throughout the European countries. This national emblem is found in the arms of Luxembourg, Belgium, Denmark, Norway, Sweden, Canada, and Ireland. Three lions are another widely used emblem. It is seen in Britain, Denmark, and Ireland. A ship is a symbol of Zebulun. It belongs mainly to Holland. Other places that have used the ship as an emblem include England, Wales, Scotland, Ireland, and Denmark. A serpent is tied to the tribe of Dan. Another emblem associated with this tribe is a horse and rider. The serpent is seldom found in any of these European countries national arms but is found in many family coats of arms. The horse is seen on shields and coat of arms in different areas of the Netherlands. The horse is also found on emblems in Denmark, England, and Scotland. The bull is the primary emblem of Ephraim. This emblem is seen in England, Denmark, and the Netherlands It is also seen in Sweden and Scotland. The second heraldic symbol of Ephraim is the unicorn. An olive branch and a bundle of arrows, which are found on the United States seal, represent Manasseh. The bundle of arrows is also found in England, Scotland, and the Netherlands. The wolf is the heraldic emblem that corresponds to Benjamin. The tribe of Benjamin was closely associated with the tribe of Judah. The Norsemen used the wolf symbol, which is tied to the "Vikings" who were part of the Saxon branch of the Scythians. Some tribes that used the wolf as a symbolic emblem migrated to Scandinavia. Some of the Norman invaders of England used the wolf as their insignia. At one time, Norway considered designating the wolf as their national emblem.[14]

Yair Davidy, world recognized authority in the field of lost Israelite identity, succinctly designates a tribe to each nation. Britain represents Ephraim. Manasseh is the USA. Rueben is the tribe for France. Simeon corresponds to the Celts and Jews. Yehuda is the tribal name that goes with the Jutes. Issachar is the tribe identified with the Swiss and Fins. Zebulun denotes Holland. Gad is the tribe associated with Sweden. Asher goes along with Scotland. Benjamin goes with Belgium and the Normans. Dan is the tribe associated with the Danes and the Celts. Naphtali are the Norwegians.[15]

Although tribal names are related to a certain country or countries, this only goes to show that a majority of each tribe tends to league together. It does not mean that each country was only comprised of one tribe. As a matter of fact, the countries of Britain, the Scandinavias, France, the Netherlands, Switzerland, Finland, and several other countries are a mixture of all the tribes of Israel, including Judah. This means that this area and the peoples descended from these countries are the people spoken of in the Bible as Jacob. I do not claim that there are not other people of Israel scattered elsewhere. What I am claiming is that these people are the pedigreed Israelites that the Bible speaks of as Jacob, Ephraim, and sometimes the house of David. Israel is often mentioned in the Bible alongside Jacob as a separate, yet related entity. There is a reason for this. Israel branched off out of Britain into countries such as Australia, Canada, South Africa, and the USA. As we shall see, the United States of America is the modern day conglomerate of the nation of Israel. Unfortunately, it is not the birthright branch of Israel.[16]

In the next chapter, I will begin an analysis of the period of Jesus Christ and the historical time period associated with him. Hopefully, it will become as clear to you as it has become to me that the entire Bible is a chronological timepiece that reveals itself in its' proper time. The time of revelation of the restoration is now.

Chapter Eight

Jesus' Mission, Commission, Prophecy and the Gospel of Paul

When Jesus arrived on the scene in Jerusalem, 400 years had elapsed between the conclusion of the Old Testament and the beginning of the New Testament. These 400 years are silent years as far as the Bible is concerned, but are full of rich history that is pertinent to Bible times. Without adding history to the pages of the Bible, we really do not understand why Jesus came. If you study the pages of the Bible and study history as well, things become understandable.[1]

At the turn of the century, from BC to AD, the Cimmerian branch of the lost Israelites, as the Gauls, Celts, and Cimry had already settled into the British Isles and France. They had also formed colonies in Denmark, Holland, Belgium and Jutland. Most, if not all, of these people were following a form of religion that was related to Hebrew in some shape or form. Many were aware of their identity.[2]

In Jerusalem, the temple had been restored and temple worship had resumed. Rome was in control of Jerusalem, as well as most of the rest of the civilized world. No descendant of the royal line of David sat on the throne in Jerusalem. The high priests that sat in seats of authority were no longer from the line of Aaron. Herod, the Great, was the king in Jerusalem at this time. He was of the lineage of Esau rather than of

Jacob. He was an evil, domineering, despotic ruler. The Jews, who were in Jerusalem, at this time, were in subjugation to this king. Legalism had become prevalent throughout the kingdom. The law had become a weapon to oppress rather than to protect the innocent. Herod was a tyrannical ruler who had no claim to the throne of David.[3]

Not one true, royal descendant of David has occupied the throne in Jerusalem since King Zedekiah.[4] Jeconias (Coniah), was the second to the last ruling king from the royal line of Solomon. A curse was placed on his lineage; as far as ruling from the throne of David in Jerusalem is concerned.[5] Zedekiah, the uncle to Coniah, rules in Jerusalem. The Babylonians come and take Zedekiah captive, and kill all of his sons. We have a dilemma here. First, Coniah is told that no man of his seed will ever sit on the throne and rule in Jerusalem again. Second, the royal line through Zedekiah is ended because his sons are all killed. When Jesus came, he claimed to be the Messiah. What did he mean?

Jesus came to seek the lost sheep of Israel. This is set forth in the book of Matthew. [6] "And when he had called unto him his twelve disciples, he gave them power against unclean spirits, to cast them out, and to heal all manner of sickness and all manner of disease".[7] "These twelve Jesus sent forth and commanded them, saying, Go not into the way of the gentiles, and into the way of the Samaritans enter Ye not: But go rather to the lost sheep of the house of Israel. And as Ye go, preach, saying The Kingdom of heaven is at hand."[8]

What Kingdom gospel did Jesus teach? He came to teach the truth of God, and to restore the fallen dynasty of David to Jerusalem. That is why he first sought the Jews, and then the lost sheep of the house of Israel. His purpose was to unite the house of Judah and the house of Israel into a United Kingdom with a king from the royal lineage of David ruling over them from Jerusalem. Jesus was the pre-destined heir, the Son of God, appointed to the throne of Jerusalem.[9]

There was one problem. Jesus came from the cursed line of Coniah (Jeconias). "And Josias begat Jeconias and his brethren, about the time they were carried away to Babylon: And after they were brought to Babylon, Jeconias begat Salathiel: And Salathiel begat Zorobabel; And Zorobabel begat Abiud: andAbiud begat Eliakim; and Eliakim begat Azor; And Azor begat Sadoc; and Sadoc begat Achim; and Achim begat Eliud; and Eliud begat Eleazar: and Eleazar begat Matthan: and Matthan begat Jacob: And Jacob begat Joseph the husband of Mary, of whom was born Jesus, who is called Christ."[10]

This problem, in itself, was solvable. God had intended that Jesus come as the perfect example for the heirs to the Kingdom to emulate. Jesus was to die, rise to life on the third day, and then rule as King of kings, Lord of lords over the house of Jacob, in a resurrected, spiritual body, from the throne of David in Jerusalem. This would bypass the curse.[11]

One other small detail stood in the way. This detail is the stone of Israel; the rock of Christ. Take note: "Morever, brethren, I would not that Ye should be ignorant, how that all our fathers were under the cloud, and all passed through the sea; and were all baptized unto Moses in the cloud and in the sea; And did all eat the same spiritual drink: for they drank of that spiritual rock that followed them: and that Rock was Christ."[12]

Jesus was the human prototype of that rock. That rock was unyielding and strong, yet it gave spiritual drink to those in need of God's strength and protection.[13] The smitten rock was a part of God's plan. Jesus knew that he was going to have to die for his people. He died so that Israel could live. The origin of this plan is stated in Exodus. "And the Lord said unto Moses, Go on before the people, and take with thee of the elders of Israel; and thy rod, wherewith thou smotest the river, take in thine hand, and go. Behold, I will stand before thee there upon the rock in Horeb; and thou shalt smite the rock, and there shall come water out of it, that the people may drink. And Moses did so in the sight of the elders of Israel."[14]

The problem is Moses later disobeyed and struck the rock two more times. This is recorded in the book of Numbers. Moses was instructed to speak to the rock that had already been smitten. "And Moses lifted up his hand, and with his rod he smote the rock twice: and the water came out abundantly, and the congregation drank, and their beasts also."[15]

Do you understand the connection? The rock was to be struck once. When Moses was instructed to later speak to the rock this was to signify that the stricken Messiah had risen and returned to rule over all Israel-both houses. Jesus was to be resurrected, return and reign as King of kings and Lord of lords. Instead, Moses struck the rock two more times.[16] This is why the Bible, at times, does not make sense. And this is why the two witnesses must come.[17]

Jesus knew that his Kingdom would not arrive on earth in his time. Notice his commission to Peter, when the church of Christ was initiated. Jesus spoke to his disciples…

"He saith unto them, But whom saith Ye that I am? And Simon Peter answered and said, Thou art the Christ, the son of the living God. And Jesus answered and said, unto him, Blessed art thou, Simon Barjona: for flesh and blood hath not revealed it unto thee, but my Father which is in heaven. And I say also unto thee, Thou art Peter, and upon this rock I will build my church; and the gates of hell shall not prevail against it. And I will give unto thee the keys of the Kingdom of heaven: and whatsoever thou shalt loose on earth shall be loosed in heaven."[18]

What rock is Jesus referring to? Peter means small rock. Does this mean that the church of Christ is built upon Peter? Perhaps! Maybe there is dual meaning here as there is with most prophecy of the Bible. Jesus agreed with Peter that he was the Christ. Christ means anointed. Remember the stone of Israel, the Christ rock, the bethel rock of Jacob? That rock was also anointed. That rock was in the area where Peter was commissioned to do most of his ministry. Coincidence? Perhaps! That rock was to shepherd at least a portion of the descendents of Jacob.[19]

Peter's commission from Jesus was to go to the lost sheep of Israel. After the first twelve years of Peter's ministry, in Palestine, Peter spent a great deal of time in the British Isles. He was following Jesus' command to go to the lost sheep. In a subsequent chapter, I will present evidence that the stone of Israel was in the British Isles at Peter's time.

When the Jews rejected Jesus, he sought the lost sheep of the house of Israel. Remember the two houses had separated in Solomon's time. There was the house of Judah and there was the house of Israel. Jesus sent his twelve disciples to the British Isles, France, Holland, Jutland, Spain and even Italy. The United Kingdom plan was put on hold It will remain that way until the two anointed witnesses, from the prophetic combination of genetic lineage come forward. They will begin the restoration of the Kingdom and the temple in Jerusalem, so all things will be ready when Jesus returns. Is this starting to make sense?

Let us move on to some specific prophecy that Jesus fulfilled. There are many hundreds of Biblical prophecies in the Bible that relate to a concept of a Messiah. I will set forth examples of a few.

The first example is found in Isaiah. "When at first he lightly afflicted the land of Zebulon and the land of Naphtali, and afterward did more grievously afflict her by the way of the sea, beyond Jordan, in Galilee of the nations. The people that walked in darkness have seen a great light: they that dwell in the land of the shadow of death, upon them hath the light shined. For unto us a child is born, unto us a son is given: and he shall receive the law upon him to keep it; and his name is called from old, Wonderful, Counselor, Eloah, The mighty, Abiding to Eternity, The messiah, because peace shall be multiplied on us in his days."[20]

This prophecy was fulfilled when Jesus came, as I will show you. It also has duel application that gives information as to what countries the two witnesses have descended from. Before I go into this, let me show a few more prophecies that Jesus made mention of.

Another example is found in Matthew. " Think not that I have come to destroy the law, or the prophets: I am not come to destroy, but to fulfill. For verily I say unto you, Til heaven and earth pass, one jot or one tittle shall in no wise pass from the law, til all be fulfilled."[21]

A third example… "That it might be fulfilled which was spoken by Esaias the prophet, saying, Behold my servant, whom I have chosen; my beloved, in whom my soul is well pleased: I will put my spirit upon him, and he shall shew judgement to the gentiles. He shall not strive, nor cry: neither shall any man hear his voice in the streets."[22]

Jesus came and fulfilled all of these prophecies. What is significant is that many prophecies that Jesus mentions are also prophetic utterances pertaining to the future.

A prophesy that relates to the coming two witnesses is also reiterated in Matthew. "And leaving Nazareth, he came and dwelt in Capernaum, which is upon the sea coast, in the borders of Zabulon and Nephthalium: That it might be fulfilled which was spoken by Esaias the prophet, saying, The land of Zabulon and the land of Nephthalium, by the way of the sea, beyond Jordan, Galilee of the gentiles: The people which sat in darkness saw great light; and to them which sat in the region and shadow of death light is sprung up."[23]

This prophecy was fulfilled partly in Jesus. Jesus mentions it specifically in allusion to the coming two witnesses, "the lampstands" if you recall. From the last chapter, Yair Davidy associates Zebulon with the Netherlands and Naphtali with Norway. The two witnesses who come have strong genetic ancestry from these two countries. One witness is of strong Dutch descent. The other witness is of strong Norwegian descent.[24]

Another prophetic utterance from Jesus that pertains to the end of this age is this…"the stone which the builders rejected, the same is become the head of the corner: this is the Lord's doing, and it is marvelous in our eyes. Therefore say I unto you, The Kingdom of God shall be taken from you, and given to a nation bringing forth the fruits thereof. And whosoever shall fall on this stone shall be broken; but on whomsoever it shall fall, it will grind him to powder."[25]

This is the stone of Israel. The people connected with it are the body of Christ; the true church. Keep your eye on this stone, shepherd AKA; the stone of destiny.[25] It has recently changed hands. It now sits in Scotland after being the property of the British in England for 700 years. Scotland is now setting up their own parliament. I expect to see a political coalition begin the Scandinavian countries, Scotland, Wales, and England if they decide against joining the Euro-dollar.

I will conclude this chapter with the gospel of Paul and the relationship with the Scythian invasions into England, as well as the later Viking invasions. Paul's ministry begins in the book of Acts. His epistles go on through the completion of the book of Hebrews. Peter all but disappears from view until he writes the Epistle of Peter. Paul became the god of the New Testament.[27]

Many Christians have built their entire belief system on what Paul said, or what they think he said. This is where the gospel of grace began with liberty to believers.[28] Christians, especially, in this country have used his gospel as an excuse to sin. What they don't seem to understand, is that this gospel was to bring a pagan people into the church of Christ. We are not a pagan country. At least we never used to be, until we took the liberty upon ourselves to reconvert to paganism. The gospel of Paul, many times, takes the entirety of the rest of the Bible out of context. It is time for the seekers of the truth to wake up to the times, realize that Paul was not God; he was not a prophet, and he may not have even been an apostle.

Who was Paul? [29] He was not one of the original Apostles selected by Jesus that were instructed to seek the lost sheep of Israel. He never met Jesus in life. He referred to himself as an apostle while Peter called him brother. There was dissension between Peter and Paul, as well as dissension between Paul and many others. Paul was an initiator of misunderstanding that may have led a great multitude of people into deception. This is what the Apostle Peter has to say…

"Nevertheless we, according to his promise, look for new heavens and a new earth, wherein dwelleth righteousness. Wherefore, beloved, seeing that Ye look for such things, be diligent that Ye may be found of him in peace, without spot, and blameless. And account that the Longsuffering of our Lord is salvation; even as our beloved brother Paul also according to the wisdom given unto him hath written unto you; As also in all his epistles, speaking in them of these things; in which are some things hard to be understood, Which they that are unlearned and unstable wrest, as they do also the other scriptures, unto their own destruction. Ye therefore, beloved, seeing Ye know these things before, beware lest Ye also, being led away with the error of the wicked, fall from your own steadfastness."[30]

Paul came as a minister to the gentiles. What exactly does gentile mean? Gentile can mean any people other than the Jew. It can also mean heathen or pagan. So there are broad applications as to the ministry of Paul. Apparently, he was sent out to Rome, Greece, Galatia, and anywhere else where there was no clear cut distinction as to what people may or may not been Israelite. He may also have converted Israelites unawares. Later, his gospel most definitely gave grace to the countless hordes of Anglo-Saxon invaders and Vikings that converted later.

The tribe of Dan settled in Greece and parts of Italy as early as 1600 BC. They traveled with descendants of Zarah, the twin brother to Pharez, son of Judah. These were part of the gentile people that Paul converted. They were also descendents of Jacob, but not necessarily Israelites out of the divided kingdom of David. Is this picture becoming clearer?

Also, the Scythian branch of the lost Israelites had not yet arrived in these Bible regions. They had separated into several bands and had become warrior nomads throughout the world. These people most certainly brought elements of other races and other cultures along with them, but they were still strongly Israelite from the lost tribes. They were to arrive in successive waves. The second divergent branch of the Cimmerians was already in southern Scandinavia, Denmark, Jutland,

Belgium and Holland. Scythians arrived and pushed some of these people further south into the British Isles and France. This began approximately 400 AD. The different, but related peoples began to mix their bloodline and their culture. Eventually most become converted Christians.

The ending of the Parthian Empire may have initiated these migrations. This was a powerful ruling empire, in Iran, until 224 AD. These people are believed to be a part of the Scythians. These Parthian warriors were forced from Iran and infiltrated into the Scandinavias during the next 100 or more years.

Approximately 700 AD. the Vikings began their reign of terror. These were a sea faring people that also came out of Scandinavia. Scandinavia was a transit route for all these migrations. They ran out of room and resources. The people went into other countries and took what they needed as they migrated. They also took wives. These would be considered gentiles that eventually converted to Christianity. Do you see where and why all these different people converged?

Briefly, I will explain. The stone of Israel was in the British Isles. This is the Christ rock. This is the rock that Jesus built his church upon.[31] Jutes, Danes, Angles, Saxons, Vikings, tribe of Dan, and Zarah, Judah all traveled through the British Isles. They fought wars to rule, they intermarried, and their cultures became thoroughly intertwined. This was God's work from start to finish. These people have become the Galilee of the gentiles that Jesus mentioned. These people have become the fullness of the gentiles that Paul mentions in Romans 11. They were all baptized into Christ.

In my next chapter, I will begin an analysis of the Biblical tribe of Judah. This tribe did not all go to Babylon. This tribe did not all return to Jerusalem. They did not all convert to Judaism. They did not die out. This tribe grew strong in power and in number throughout the world. And, this tribe converged in these same areas; the British Isles and Scandinavia.

Chapter Nine

The Tribe(s) of Judah?

Who all is of the tribe of Judah – particularly the descendants of Nathan and the royal line of Solomon? While the "house of Judah" comprises the southern division of the divided kingdom of the dynasty of David, the people of Judah are more widespread than this. In a previous chapter, Biblical evidence has been provided that shows that a good proportion of Judah was taken into Assyrian captivity with the northern division of the divided kingdom. All of Judah did not go into Babylonian captivity. As well as the people of Judah from the Davidic kingdom era, there were other people of Judah sailing the seas and colonizing cities elsewhere. Let me recapitulate a promise given through Jacob to his son, Judah.

"Judah, thou art he whom thy brethren shall praise: thy hand shall be in the neck of thine enemies; thy father's children shall bow down before thee. Judah is a lion's whelp: from the prey, my son, thou art gone up: he stooped down, he couched as a lion; who shall rouse him up? The sceptre shall not depart from Judah, nor a lawgiver from between his feet, until Shiloh come; and unto him shall the gathering of the people be."[1]

The sceptre is an emblem of authority. Judah is to hold the sceptre down throughout the history of the world. From the time of King David, there has been a royal line of descent from the lineage of Judah.

At the time of Jerusalem's' fall, this line diverged. The branch of Jeconias (the cursed king) went into Babylonian captivity, after which, Zedekiah, the uncle to Jeconias, ruled in Jerusalem. The line of Zedekiah continued but the throne of David was moved out of Jerusalem and placed elsewhere. Jacob's prophecy states that the sceptre will remain with Judah (the royal line) until Shiloh comes. Then the sceptre will change hands. Some say that Shiloh is the Messiah (Jesus), and at his Second Coming this prophecy will be fulfilled. Let me expound on the history of Judah before any inferred conclusions are formed.

There is a little know story in the Bible about a breach of the line of Judah.[2] This is in Genesis. It's an extremely relevant portion of Bible history that should not be neglected. "And it came to pass in the time of her travail, that behold, twins were in the womb. And, it came to pass, as he drew back his hand, that, behold, his brother came out: and she said, How hast thou broken forth? this breach be upon thee: therefore his name was called Pharez. And afterward came out his brother, that had the scarlet thread upon his hand: and his name was called Zarah."[3]

This would not have been mentioned if it was not a necessary piece to the understanding of the Bible and its logical conclusion. What people may not know is that Pharez, the son of Judah, has been the Biblical royal line throughout the pages of the Bible. The Jews came from this line. King David came from this line. [4]

It appears from scripture that the Zarah branch of Judah was the firstborn, or was meant to be. Zarah never ruled during the time of David or Solomon. At least their kingdoms are not recorded in the Bible as the kingdoms that ruled under the sovereignty of God. The Kings of the Bible came from the Pharez branch of Judah. Somewhere, along the line, Zarah was meant to reign. The breach between Pharez and Zarah was mended through a union between descendants of David, and an already established line of Kings from the Zarah line.[5]

Solomon was the son through which the primary royal line of David was established. This royal lineage was the line, in Jerusalem, through which all the Kings of Judah descended. A divergence occurred after Jeconias (the cursed king) ruled. This line went into Babylonian captivity. Many from this line, and tribe, went back to Jerusalem after the Babylonian exile was over. Because of this curse, no heir has ever sat on the throne of David, in Jerusalem, and ruled since.

One more king ruled in Jerusalem after this. This was King Zedekiah, the uncle to Jeconias. Eventually his sons were all killed, his eyes were put out, and he was placed in a Babylonian prison. This was to keep any royal heirs from having authority again.

What was not counted on was that, by Hebrew law, a daughter could perpetuate the royal line.[6] This is exactly what happened, according to Biblical scripture. It is recorded in the book of Jeremiah.

"But Johanan, the son of Kareah, and all the captains of the forces, took all the remnant of Judah, that were returned from all the nations, whither they had been driven, to dwell in the land of Judah; Even men, and women, and children, and the king's daughters, and every person that Nebuzar-adan the captain of the guard had left with Gadaliah the son of Ahikam, the son of Shaphan, and Jeremiah the prophet, and Baruch the son of Neriah. So they came into the land of Egypt: for they obeyed not the voice of the LORD : thus came they even to Tahpanhes."[7]

The Bible does not say how many daughters King Zedekiah had. They traveled with the prophet Jeremiah and his writer companion Baruch. This is recorded in Jeremiah. After their journey to Egypt, the Bible becomes silent on their whereabouts. When one looks at this logically, it makes sense. To reveal the whereabouts of the remaining lineage of the royal line of Solomon would have sealed their fate.[8]

There are several Irish and Scottish stories stating that the royal line came to Ireland. One of these, from ancient Irish record, makes reference to a King's daughter, a prophet, and his companion Baruch. They all arrived in Ireland at approximately the same time, 584 BC. This is the same time that the kingdom of Jerusalem fell. In their possession they brought ancient treasures from the kingdom of David, which included a chest, a harp, and a stone called a Lia-Fail. This was none other than the stone of Israel; the bethel stone. They apparently arrived in Ireland via a sea route; escorted and helped by the tribe of Dan who were seafaring travelers. During the time of Nebuchadnezzar, the remnant, which included Jeremiah, Baruch, and the King's daughters, had to flee Egypt. Apparently, some of the tribe of Zarah, Judah and the tribe of Dan rescued them from the wrath of Nebuchadnezzar and brought them into a secluded Irish kingdom. They came by sea into Scotland then into Ireland. [9]

This early Irish kingdom is believed to have been established by the Tuatha De Danann in a place called Tara. Tara was the inauguration and burial site for ancient Irish kings. In Tara, at very early dates, feasts were held. These feasts, quite possibly were the Levitical Holy days that were a symbol of Judaic and Hebrew religion. This is where the king's daughter(s) arrived with Jeremiah and the stone.

After their arrival in Ireland, one of Zedekiah's daughters married into the royal line of this kingdom, supposedly a prince from the line of Zarah Judah. It is in this manner that the breach is healed between Pharez and Zarah. The royal line continues.[10]

There are other similar variations to this story. I do not feel that it is necessary to elaborate on them all since they all relay the same basic tale, and they all confirm that "the stone" arrived in Ireland about 584 BC. Kings have been crowned on this stone ever since.

In an earlier chapter, I cited several sources showing how the Cimmerians arrived in northwest and northern Europe between approximately 600-300 BC. The branch that migrated northward into Jutland, Denmark, the Netherlands, and Norway began to arrive about the year 525 BC. This was about sixty years after the royal remnant arrived in Ireland, and parts of these same areas. These may have been a large degree of Judah, as well. Many of them may have been descendants of Nathan, son of David. Nathan was to remain loyal to Solomon. Those of Nathan, who did not go into Babylonian captivity, may have decided to follow the "waymarks" and locate predecessors.

Who was Nathan? Nathan was a son of David born prior to Solomon. Nathan is also mentioned as a prophet in conjecture with Zadok the priest and Benaiah in the anointing of Solomon. Nathan was a servant to his brother. And, Nathan is of the line of promise.[11]

There may have been a breach, of sorts, between Solomon and Nathan. Although Nathan supports Solomon and stands with him, Nathan may have been the line through which the royal line was meant to come. In the New Testament, there are two lines given for Christ. One is of the branch of Jeconias, descendant of Solomon. The other is of the branch of Nathan. This has puzzled scholars for some time. The solution may be simpler than it appears. This is prophecy waiting to be fulfilled. In due time, it will be!

As I have tried to portray, the royal line of David did not end in Jerusalem, Egypt or Babylon. It continued into Ireland, Britain, Scotland, and Scandinavia where there were already kingdoms of the Zarah Judah branch. Zarah, as I said before, was the twin brother to Pharez, who was the son of Judah. Throughout the ruling kingdoms of the Bible, Pharez is always mentioned as being the progenitor of the royal line. Little is outstanding about Zarah. Although it is little known, Zarah did colonize many areas, and mysteriously, they seem to be mentioned in conjunction with the Israelite tribe of Dan. They traveled together in ships from the time before Moses. If they have been together in close proximity, since this time, it is only natural that they intermarried and merged into one people. The tribe of Dan, along with descendants of Zarah, had established colonies and kingdoms throughout Scandinavia, Ireland, and Scotland by the time that David was crowned King in Jerusalem. [12] They had a highly advanced civilization and were a highly educated people. Scriptural support for the merging of these two groups of Jacob's descendants is found in the Bible.

The first example is given to Judah from Jacob. "Judah is a lion's whelp: from thy prey, my son, thou art gone up: he stooped down, he couched as a lion, and as an old lion; who shall rouse him up?" [13]

The second example is found in a prophecy stated by Moses to the tribe of Dan. "Dan is a lion's whelp: he shall leap from Bashan."[14]

From these prophecies, it appears that these two (Dan and Zarah), somewhere along the line, became one. What is interesting is that many of the heraldic emblems of Britain, Denmark, Norway, Sweden, Scotland, and several other related European countries have lions in their blazon and heraldic arms. Coincidence? I hardly think so.

As to a merging between Naphtali, Dan and some lineage of Judah (perhaps Nathan), research has been conducted that supports this. According to Yair Davidy an expert in the field of lost Israelite identity, and I quote…"Along with the Scythian movement northward the Cadussi had apparently relocated themselves which explains their identification afterwards with the Naphtalites east of the Urals. Chinese records record a group named "Yautya" together with the Naphtali. According to the Chinese, the "Yatya" were a section of Naphtali also referred to as "Hu" and as "Yeda." The Assyrians had termed Judaens of Judah and of Sma'al in Cilicia, "Yaeti" and "Yadi" which names are similar to the appellations "Yatya" and "Yeda" for the group amongst the Naphtalites. Similarly, in Caucasian dialects "Yat" or "Yet" means Jew. The Naphtalite Yaeti seem to correspond to the Yautya who formally had been situated in Gadrosia and had there adjoined the Dangalai. The Dangalai have a name implying Dan of the Galilee" (Davidy). [15]

The Naphtali is the tribe that settled primarily in Norway. Evidence is documented that shows Judah traveled with these people, and to this country, as well as to surrounding countries. What may not be quite as apparent is that different branches of Judah converged in a relatively small area of European countries from 1000 BC – at least 700AD. There are implications here that should not be ignored. Recall the promise from God, through the prophet Nathan, to David- I will build thee a house.[16]

Chapter Ten

Ephraim

Before I get into the topic of the "house of David" I am going to touch upon an explanation for the concept of Ephraim. I say concept because Ephraim is mentioned over and over again in the Bible. It is a broad word that encompasses much. Ephraim has varied meaning, but after unveiling all the differing hues, a specific becomes quite clear. Ephraim is the birthright aggregate of nations, and the people that go with it.

A general definition of Ephraim begins with the northern division of the divided kingdom of David. Remember that the kingdom of Israel was divided into the "house of Judah" and the "house of Israel." The house of Israel was sometimes referred to as the house of Joseph or the house of Ephraim. This is the part of the kingdom that went into Assyrian captivity. This is the part of Israel that lost its identity and became not a people. This is the wandering group that not only lost their identity but their religion as well. This is the lost group that Jesus came to seek. Let us see what the Bible has to say about Ephraim.

"Behold, I will bring them from the north country, and gather them from the coasts of the earth, and with them the blind and the lame, the woman with child and her that travaileth with child together: a great company shall return thither. They shall come with weeping, and with supplications will I lead them: I will cause them to walk by the rivers of waters in a straight way, wherein they shall not stumble: for I am a father to Israel, and Ephraim is my firstborn."[1]

Ephraim is shown here as the birthright branch of Israel returning to Zion in the last days.[2] Ephraim must be re-united with the house of Judah in Jerusalem. This is sure prophecy. Ezekiel confirms this specifically.

"Morever, thou son of man, take thee one stick, and write upon it, For Judah, and for the children of Israel his companions: then take another stick, and write upon it, For Joseph, the stick of Ephraim, and for all the house of Israel his companions: and join them one to another into one stick; and they shall become one in thine hand."[3]

This prophecy is further expounded: "And say unto them, Thus saith the Lord God; Behold I will take the children of Israel from among the heathen, whither they be gone, and will gather them on every side, and bring them into their own land: and I will make them one nation in the land upon the mountains of Israel; and one king shall be king to them all: and they shall be no more two nations, neither shall they be divided into two kingdoms any more at all."[4]

There is more scriptural support to help identify Ephraim. "Is Ephraim my dear son? is he a pleasant child? for since I spake against him, I do earnestly remember him still: therefore my bowels are troubled for him; I will surely have mercy upon him, saith the Lord. Set thee up waymarks, make thee high heaps: set thine heart toward the highway, even the way which thou wentest: turn again, o virgin of Israel, turn again to these thy cities."[5]

Stone monuments have been found in Ireland, France, Britain, the Netherlands, and Scandinavia that are of identical design to the type found throughout Israel. Could these be the waymarks mentioned in Jeremiah's prophecy? Jeremiah was a prophet, so the prophet must be proved true. These stone heaps were set up to identify Ephraim and to lead Ephraim home.[6]

According to Yair Davidy, world recognized authority in the field of lost Israelite identity, the historical dating of these stone megalithic monuments may have been set too early. "In archaeological and historical studies of Western Europe dolmens are associated with the Celtic Druids. Wherever Celts and Druids were found, together, so too were these dolmens."[7]

Zechariah also gives evidence to support the idea of Ephraim returning home after a long interval. "And I will strengthen the house of Judah and I will save the house of Joseph, and I will bring them again to place them; for I have mercy upon them: and they shall be as though I had not cast them off: for I am the Lord their God, and I will hear them. And they of Ephraim shall be like a mighty man, and their heart shall rejoice as through wine: yea their children shall see it, and be glad: their heart shall rejoice in the lord. I will hiss for them and gather them: for I have redeemed them."[8]

From the foregoing scriptural support, evidence has been presented those points out Ephraim. Ephraim is the northern division of the whole house of Israel. It is sometimes referred to as the house of Joseph. It is sometimes referred to as Jacob. In this study, we shall examine how Ephraim is a separate, yet related, branch off of the trunk of Joseph. In other words, all of Ephraim comes from Joseph. Not all of Joseph is Ephraim.[9] Let's begin this with an overview of what Ephraim covers.

The word Ephraim denotes royalty. It conjures up images of eloquence and nobility. For this very reason it has always been associated with Britain. The British have always been associated with the aristocrats of high birth. But Britain is not the only nation of these surrounding countries that are of royalty.[10]

A better description of Ephraim might be regal leadership in the hands of monarchs. This definition would give credence to the whole arena of Ephraim- N. Ireland, Wales, Scotland, England, Denmark, Norway, and Sweden. Remember that Ephraim was to become a company of nations from which kings descend. These are the company of nations that are the aristocrats. These countries will stand together (not always by choice). This is Ephraim. [1]

Sometimes in the Bible, we see Jacob mentioned in conjunction with Israel. There is a reason for this. Israel is usually the second entity after Jacob. Reference to Israel has to do with parts of England and its main offshoot; America. Jacob is identified by its close proximity to the Bethel stone. This is the stone of destiny, Jacob's pillar, or the shepherd of Israel. It is an identifying mark to clarify who Jacob is. [12]

In 1996, the stone of destiny was moved from England back to Scotland. [13] Previously, this stone sat in England for 700 years and was used in the coronation of all its British monarchs. It's interesting to note that this stone was anointed by Jacob, and was designated God's house. Power, from God, was to follow that stone. It is also interesting to note, as a point of reference, the power that Britain has maintained over the years as a military leader of the world. If you care to speculate, what will become of their power now? And what will become of the power of the United States of America. Time will reveal all.

This author believes that Ephraim and Jacob are interchangeable. If this is the case, Ephraim is not a title for any one country but, rather, a title for all the related countries- and lineage- of a specified area. My thoughts concerning this subject go forward as this…

Jacob was the name of the father of the twelve tribes of Israel. Later, Jacob's name was changed to Israel. Jacob is the conglomerate of all twelve tribes of Israel. Jacob comes before Israel and is therefore the birthright branch of Israel. Do you understand this connection? Jacob is the firstborn of Israel. Jacob is Ephraim.

The other branch of Israel is Manasseh. [14] This branch came through Jacob, settled in England, and then overflowed into the United States of America, South Africa, Canada, Australia, and several other countries. This happened when the later Scythian invasions took place after the time of Jesus Christ. The Scythian branch mixed with the Cimmerians and then passed over.

For many years, Britain and the United States have ruled the world. This may all be coming to an end. The reason for this is reiterated over and over again in the Bible. Disobedience and rejection of the word of God will be their downfall.[15]

"the stone which the builders rejected, the same is become the head of the corner: this is the Lord's doing, and it is marvelous in our eyes. Therefore say I unto you, The kingdom of God shall be taken from you, and given to a nation bringing forth the fruits thereof. And whosoever shall fall on this stone shall be broken; but on whomsoever it shall fall, it will grind him to powder."[16]

Chapter Eleven

House of David

The topic of the house of David may well prove to be the key of the Bible that unlocks the remainder of the history of this era. Many people believe that the house of David will not be restored until the full restoration of all the seed of Israel to Jerusalem. This is incorrect. The house of David has existed from the time of Jesus.[1] What I intend to do, in this chapter, is to show that this house has been around for quite some time, and it's inhabitants come from a relatively small area of the world. The house of David is a separate, yet related, entity of the house of Joseph from the other two houses. It is not the house of Judah and it is only a portion of the house of Israel. God promised David that he would build him a house. If you believe the Bible, this prophecy must have been fulfilled.[2]

To begin, I will reiterate a Biblical promise given to David. This promise came through Nathan to David. It is an established fact:

"And it came to pass the same night, that the word of God came to Nathan, saying, Go and tell David my servant, Thus saith the Lord, Thou shalt not build me an house to dwell in: For I have not dwelt in an house since the day that I brought up Israel unto this day: but have gone from tent to tent, and from one tabernacle to another."[3]

"And it shall come to pass, when thy days be expired that thou must go to be with thy fathers, that I will raise up thy seed after thee, which shall be of thy sons; and I will establish his Kingdom. He shall build me an house, and I will establish his throne forever. I will be his father, and he shall be my son: and I will not take my mercy away from him, as I took it from him that was before thee: But I will settle him in mine house and in mine kingdom for ever: and his throne shall be established for evermore."[4]

II Samuel has a slightly different version of this same promise. For comparison purposes, I feel that I should include this...

"And when thy days be fulfilled, and thou shalt sleep with thy fathers, I will set up thy seed after thee, which shall proceed out of thy bowels, and I will establish his kingdom for ever. I will be his father, and he shall be my son. If he commit iniquity, I will chasten him with the rod of men, and with the stripes of the children of men: but my mercy shall not depart away from him, as I took it from Saul, whom I put away before thee: thy throne shall be established for ever."[5]

This is an unconditional promise. Unconditional means that nothing can alter the terms of the agreement. It is a promise that is not restricted by rules. Human failure or sin cannot change this promise. It guarantees a house and a kingdom will be established through David's lineage.

This kingdom is to be a perpetual dynasty. Although there is spiritual application here, this kingdom is to also be an everlasting, temporal kingdom on earth. Somewhere, right now, this kingdom exists. This kingdom includes an established house. House, in this context, would mean a family that includes ancestors, descendants and kindred. This house of David is to be a group of people of the lineage of David through Nathan and Solomon. This makes absolute sense because the promise came through Nathan. Considering that this promise did come through Nathan, I am going to suggest that somewhere, right now, a group of people exist that have been given an unconditional, hereditary entitlement. This entitlement includes mercy, a house, and an everlasting kingdom. Did Jesus build that house? [6]

First of all, Jesus was of the lineage of David. According to the New Testament, Jesus was born of the line of Solomon as well as of the line of Nathan. (Scripture also says Jesus was adopted by Joseph who was of the line of David). So, Jesus does fit the profile of the Son of God who would come and establish an everlasting kingdom for God. But, the questions here are…was this kingdom a spiritual kingdom of another realm and domain?[7] Or is this kingdom a corporeal, ever present physical dynasty on earth? Although I believe in a spiritual side to this kingdom, this work deals mainly with a here and now kingdom, and the history of that kingdom. Looking at the Bible realistically, most of the Bible is a literary, historical journey down through time with occasional periods of supernatural intervention. To spiritualize the entire book detracts from the overall message and we miss the main point. As to the question, did Jesus build this house? My answer is yes. Jesus built the house of David. He set the church in motion and uttered prophecy pertinent to the fulfillment of this house becoming complete. An example of this is found in Revelation…

"And to the angel of the church in Philadelphia write: These things saith he that is holy, he that is true, he hath the key of David, he that openeth, and no man shutteth; and shutteth, and no man openeth; I know thy works: behold, I have set before thee an open door, and no man can shut it: for thou hast a little strength, and hast kept my word, and has not denied my name. Behold, I will make them of the synagogue of Satan, which say they are Jews, and are not, but do lie; behold, I will make them to come and worship before thy feet, and to know that I have loved thee. Because thou hast kept the word of my patience, I will also keep thee from the hour of temptation, which shall come upon the world, to try them that dwell upon the earth."[8]

The house that Jesus built is the house of David. That house is also Jacob.[9] And this house is given exemption from the time of great tribulation that is coming to test the rest of the world.

"Alas! for the day is great, so that none is like it: it is even the time of Jacob's Trouble; but he shall be saved out of it."[10]

At this point, I am going to detour a bit from the main topic of this chapter, the house of David. The reason for this has to do with an agreement made to Solomon that was conditional. This concurrent covenant gets a little tricky as far as the identity of Israel is concerned in relationship to the house of David. Let me proceed cautiously. The covenant between God and Solomon goes as follows...

"And as for thee, if thou wilt walk before me, as David thy father walked, and do according to all that I have commanded thee, and shalt observe my statutes and my judgements, Then will I stablish the throne of thy kingdom, according as I have covenanted with David thy father, saying, There shall not fail thee a man to be ruler in Israel. But if ye turn away, and forsake my statutes and my commandment, which I have set before you, and shall go and serve other gods, and worship them; Then will I pluck them up by the roots out of my land, which I have given them; and this house, which I have sanctified for my name, I will cast out of my sight, and will make it to be a proverb and a byword among all nations."[11]

From these Biblical verses it is clear that the promise to Solomon was conditional. The royal line of Solomon was guaranteed a man to rule in Israel if these men followed the laws of God. Solomon failed. Israel separated into two kingdoms. Captivity and hardship followed. Israel disappeared into obscurity. The whereabouts of the ten-tribed house of Israel was cast into obscurity because of the prophecy of God. Israel indeed became a byword throughout the world.

Israel did resurface unbeknownst to the majority of all involved. After the Assyrian captivity, and then after the time of Jesus Christ, the Scythian invasions took place in Europe. These were a huge multitude of warrior people from the tribes of Israel that invaded Europe and overflowed into Britain. Britain became Israel. Solomon's throne (the stone of destiny) found its way to the British Isles. A descendant of

Solomon once again ruled from that throne. Israel was promised an additional country. The population grew. The people of Britain overflowed and the United States of America was born. America became the Manasseh branch of the house of Israel. From this brief synopsis, we see that Solomon's descendants continually failed. In my next chapter, I will explain how, once again, the throne of Solomon has been moved and rejected. For now, let me focus back in on the house of David.

The house of David was to have distinguishing characteristics to identify it. One of these characteristics was that kings would rule. Another characteristic of the house of David is that it is to exercise compassionate, righteous rulership. Another characteristic of this house is that it would be a servant to Solomon. Let me illustrate these characteristics further.[12]

The first characteristic of the house of David I want to expound upon is that kings would come from this group of people.[13] Kings have been a part of Europe from before the time of Jesus. Denmark has one of the oldest constitutional monarchies in the world. Norway has been a nation of kings from way back. Sweden is another country that has treasured their privileged heritage down through time. The British Isles, Northern Ireland, Scotland and England have fought wars for their crown. There is Biblical support for this promise. "And God said unto him, I am God Almighty: be fruitful and multiply; a nation and a company of nations shall be of thee, and kings shall come out of thy loins."[14] A second characteristic of the house of David is that it is to exercise righteous, compassionate leadership.[15] Britain vies for this capacity but has never been "totally" successful. (Britain is a constituent of the house of David). At this point in history, the only countries that can truly claim this ability are Denmark, Norway and Sweden. These three countries are known for their just and compassionate leadership and treatment of their subjects. The kings of these countries serve their people without pretensions of superiority. That is what has made these kingdoms successful. This is a major area for the gathering of Nathan's descendants. A third characteristic of the house of David is that this house would be a servant to Solomon. When all is said and done, who has supported the Jews, as well as the monarchy of Britain, since their conversion to Christianity? Although the United States can claim this role; will their staunch continue? The Bible states this:

"And the king hath sent with him Zadok the priest, and Nathan the prophet, and Benaiah the son of Jehoiada, and the Cherethites, and the Pelethites, and they have caused him to ride upon the king's mule: And Zadok the priest and Nathan the prophet have anointed him king in Gihon: and they are come up from thence rejoicing, so that the city rang again. This is the noise that ye have heard. And also Solomon sitteth on the throne of the kingdom."[16]

This is history and this is prophecy. In the time of David, Nathan stood behind Solomon. At this time, Scandinavia (particularly Norway) stands behind Britain, the United States, and the state of Israel.

"The people of Denmark on the whole belong to Dan but Judah was also prominent along with the presence of other tribes. When the Germans conquered Denmark they ordered all the Jews to wear the star of David. So the king of Denmark put one on himself and ordered his subjects to do the same."[17]

As well as their unwavering support for the Jews, the Scandinavians, particularly Norway, have always supported the British and it's monarchy. They have supported their decisions and often they have repaired their blunders without self- exaltation. These people remain an enigma to historians, but their identity is gradually unfolding.[18]

Scandinavia was once a transit route. It is an area in Europe where all twelve tribes of Israel traveled. This area is where a large number from the tribe of Dan converged with a large number from the tribe of Ephraim. It is an area of Europe where the Zarah branch of Judah intermarried with the royal line of Solomon. It is also the conglomerate of countries where the Nathan line of Pharez Judah converged with the other royal Solomon line of David as well as the Zarah branch of Judah.

Other tribes of Israel mixed into the frame of this group and became constituents of it. Dan, Naphtali, Gad, and Judah make up the foundation of this area. Let me expound on this a bit.

The house of David was once a large transit route through North and Northwest Europe. The Cimmerian descendants had already settled in Northern Ireland, Wales, Scotland, Denmark, Norway, and the Netherlands at a very early date BC. A good majority of these early settlers were of the tribe of Judah. Later, the Scythian branch of the Israelites came through these areas.

"Scandinavia was destined to serve as a place of settlement for many of the Scythian peoples and as an area of transit for others on their way west. A clarification of Scandinavia's history facilitates the explanation of Scandinavia's historical role. Several distinct periods are observable: 1) The Bronze Age 2) The era between 100bce and 100ce in which Scandinavia was repopulated especially by Royal Scyths and Goths 3) A century of disturbance (300's- 400's ce) in which Scandinavia was apparently conquered and in which many tribes left and headed further west 4) The arrival of new peoples from east Scythia in the 500's and 600's culminated in the 700's experiencing overpopulation and unsettlement which led to the Viking oversea expeditions."[19]

From this, it should be clear that these fore-mentioned countries became a mixture of all twelve tribes of Israel. Judah was a pre-dominant tribe in Northern Ireland, Scotland, Wales, Denmark, Holland, Norway, and Sweden. With this Judaic foundation, we have a basis for the house of David.

"It is noticeable that quite often the tribes of Naphtali and Dan were interwoven and that both appear to have been present in the Scythian Naphtalite group. Another section of the Naphtali were known as Ye-da or Ye-ta which is similar to variations on the name of Judah found in the North Mesopotamian area."[20] Naphtali pertains to Norway and Dan pertains to Denmark. Also, according to Yair Davidy, "An Aramaic inscription mentions a "house of David" somehow in connection with Dan in the Galilee."[21]

Let me build a supposition connecting the house of David with Jacob. First of all, the lion is the national emblem in Britain, Denmark, Norway, Sweden, Scotland, Northern Ireland, and the Netherlands. The lion is the symbol of Judah. Second, the stone of Bethel, otherwise known as the stone of destiny, was to represent Jacob. From since around 500 BC, the stone of destiny has been stationed in three of these countries- Ireland, Britain, and Scotland. This to me serves as self-explanatory evidence. In my next chapter, I will show the history of the stone of destiny and how it relates to the people of Jacob. Let me conclude this chapter with a promise given to Jacob.

"And God said unto him, I am God Almighty: be fruitful and multiply: a nation and a company of nations shall be of thee, and kings shall come out of thy loins; and the land which I gave Abraham and Isaac, to thee will I give it, and to thy seed after thee will I give the land. And God went up from him in the place where he talked with him. And Jacob set up a pillar in the place where he talked with him, even a pillar of stone: and he poured a drink offering thereon, and he poured oil thereon. And Jacob called the name of the place where God spake with him, Bethel."[22]

Chapter Twelve

Is the Stone of Israel the Rock of Christ?

The stone of Israel is the most important topic of this work alongside the two witnesses. I have conducted extensive research into the plausible and possible relationship between the stone of Israel and the Rock of Christ. Many times, in the Bible, stones are mentioned. Jesus is often referred to as a rock. There has been much theological debate between scholars as to who was the rock that the church was built upon. Some say this rock was Peter, while others conclude that the rock was Jesus. Perhaps we have all misinterpreted the metaphor. What if the church was built upon an actual rock? 1Talk about a literal translation of the Bible; this one beats all. But it fits. I will begin an exegetical analysis of the stone of Israel and exemplify its relevance to the history of the Bible, as well as to the rock of Christ that is addressed in the New Testament.

The stone of Israel, the ROCK, is mentioned from the beginning of the Bible and into the New Testament. It is a reliable foundation and reference point because it has outlived all the patriarchs, and it still exists. This places this rock in a position of utmost notoriety, and it should be dealt with as such. The problem is… most people have stumbled over this rock. Many examples of the stone of Israel are found in the Bible. I will shed light upon a few.

The first example is found in Exodus. "And Moses cried unto the Lord, saying, what shall I do unto this people? they be almost ready to stone me. And the Lord said unto Moses, Go on before the people, and take with thee of the elders of Israel; and thy rod, where with thou smotest the river, take in thine hand, and go. Behold, I will stand before thee there upon the rock in Horeb; and thou shalt smite the rock, and there shall come water out of it, that the people may drink. And Moses did so in the sight of the elders of Israel."[2]

A second example is found in Numbers. "And the Lord spake unto Moses, saying, Take the rod, and gather thou the assembly together, thou, and Aaron thy brother, and speak ye unto the rock before their eyes; and it shall give forth his water, and thou shalt bring forth to them water out of the rock: so thou shalt give the congregation and their beasts drink. And Moses took the rod from before the lord, as he commanded him. And Moses and Aaron gathered the congregation together before the rock, and he said unto them, Hear now, ye rebels; must we fetch you water out of this rock? And Moses lifted up his hand, and with his rod he smote the rock twice; and the water came out abundantly, and the congregation drank, and their beasts also."[3]

A third example of this rock is found in Isaiah: "Go ye forth of Babylon, flee ye from the Chaldeans, with a voice of singing declare ye, tell this, utter it even to the end of the earth; say ye, the Lord hath redeemed his servant Jacob. And they thirsted not when he led them through the deserts: he caused the waters to flow out of the rock for them: he clave the rock also, and the waters gushed out."[4]

All of these examples refer to the same rock.[5] There are more examples that tend to substantiate the validity of this rock and its importance in connection with Israel. Water came out of this rock to sustain the Israelites during their treks through the wilderness. The last example specifically mentions Jacob in concurrence with this rock. This, in itself, provides evidence as to which rock this is. Recall Jacob's Pillar, the rock of Bethel. Let's proceed with a Biblically established timeline of this pillar.

Approximately 1935 BC, Jacob had a dream. This is the stairway to heaven dream. In summary, Jacob took a stone to be his pillow. He had a dream of angels ascending and descending a ladder to and from heaven. Jacob designates the place Bethel and he also calls the stone Bethel, which means God's house. Then, in consecration, he pours oil over the stone to make it a Biblically acclaimed anointed rock.[6]

Approximately 1883 BC, the stone of Israel is with Jacob in Egypt. Jacob passes on the birthright to Joseph, which includes the stone of Israel. From Joseph, the stone is designated to come out from. It is referred to as the shepherd in Genesis. Joseph is responsible for protecting and keeping this stone.[7]

Approximately 1453 BC, the stone of Israel is with Moses. Moses, from the tribe of Levi, was chosen by God to lead the children of Israel out of Egypt.[8] When Moses took command, the shepherd stone, which was already in Egypt, went with him. God gave Moses his authority, and the rock went with that authority.

Before Moses died, he anointed Joshua to succeed him. With the lying on of hands, Moses passed the mantel of authority on to him. Joshua became the authoritative leader of the children of Israel. Along with that authority went the stone of Israel. This is recorded in the book of Joshua. It occurred in the approximate year, 1383 BC. "And Joshua said unto all the people, Behold, this stone shall be a witness unto us: for it hath heard all the words of the Lord which he spake unto us: it shall be therefore a witness unto you, lest ye deny your God."[9]

The next time we hear of the stone of Israel is in the Biblical book of Kings. The year is 798 BC. At this time, Joash is crowned king of Jerusalem. "And he brought forth the king's son, and put the crown upon him, and gave him the testimony; and they made him king, and anointed him: and they clapped their hands, and said God save the king. And when Athaliah heard the noise of the guard and of the people, she came to the people into the temple of the Lord. And when she looked, behold, the king stood by a pillar, as the manner was, and the princes and the trumpeters by the king, and all the people of the land rejoiced, and blew their trumpets."[10]

From 640 BC on, little is mentioned about this stone which is now in the possession of the royal line of Judah.[11] According to the last testimony of Jacob, in his blessing to his twelve sons, the stone is to come out from Joseph in the last days. This is certain prophecy. Let's proceed and envision what happened to this stone during the final days of the kingdom of Judah.

Jeremiah was a prophet, appointed by God, at the time of Zedekiah the last reigning king of Judah in Jerusalem. God ordained him a prophet from birth. His commission was this…

"See, I have this day set thee over the nations and over the kingdoms, to root out, and to pull down, and to destroy, and to throw down, to build, and to plant."[12]

The kingdom of David was on the verge of complete annihilation. Jeremiah was the one entrusted with the king's daughters and with the stone of Israel. He was to take them to another area and replant the empire, until Shiloh, to whom the gathering of the people should be, would appear. Along with this responsibility, Jeremiah took the Ark of the Covenant and hid it.

"It was also contained in the same writing, that the prophet, being warned of God, commanded the tabernacle and the ark to go with him, as he went forth into the mountain, where Moses climbed up, and saw the heritage of God. And when Jeremy came thither, he found an hollow cave, wherein he laid the tabernacle, and the ark, and the altar of incense, and so stopped the door. And some of those that followed him came to mark the way, but they could not find it. Which when Jeremy perceived, he blamed them, saying, As for that place, it shall be unknown until the time that God gather his people again together, and receive them unto mercy."[13]

What is known is that a stone of presumed value arrives in Ireland at the same time Judah goes into Babylonian captivity. This rock is accompanied by a prophet, a scribe, and the king's daughter in the year 584 BC.[14]

According to E. Raymond Capt, archaeologist, historian, and author of "Jacob's Pillar," the arrival of this stone to Irish soil is not baseless. "The arrival in Ireland of the Bethel stone rests upon the authority of the ancient records of Ireland and the traditions which abound there. Here let us understand that the ancient historical legends of Ireland are, generally speaking, far from being baseless myths. The Irish people are a people who eminently cling to tradition. Not only were the great happenings that marked great epochs enshrined in their memory, forever, but even little events that trivially affected the history of their race, were and are, seldom forgotten."[15]

With the arrival of Jeremiah, his scribe, and the king's daughter, with the stone of destiny, certain other relics were said to have arrived also. These included a harp and a chest. The harp is believed to have been the harp of King David.

E. Raymond Capt has more to say on the arrival of the stone, and I quote, "It rests on a succession of well authenticated Irish, Scottish, and English historical documents which may be regarded as practically undisputed. Writers on the subject, quoting from such works as "The Chronicles of Eri," "The Annals of the Four Masters," "The Annals of Clonmacnoise," etc, locate the stone originally at Tara, County of Meath, Ireland."[16]

Now that we have the stone of destiny firmly established in Ireland, what became of it? First of all, according to one legend, Tea Tephi, the daughter of King Zedekiah accompanied Jeremiah to Ireland. There she married Eochaidh, a prince of the scarlet thread; (Zarah Judah) Tea was then coronated Queen, on the stone of Bethel, in Tara, Ireland.

"In the Chronicles of Eri," by Milner, we find Eochaidh, the husband of Tea Tephi, associated with the stone Lia Fail. The account is titled, "The Story of Lia Fail" and states: "In the early days it was carried about by priests on the march in the wilderness (hence the much worn rings still attached to it, one on each end). Later it was borne by the sea from East to West- 'to the extremity of the world of the sun's going' (an expression used by the Romans to describe Britain). Its bearers had resolved, at starting, to move on the face of the waters in search of their brethren. Shipwrecked on the coast of Ireland, they yet came safe with Lia Fail... Eochaidh sent a car for Lia Fail, and he himself was placed thereon."[17]

From approximately 584 BC until 500 AD, the stone of destiny is in Ireland. During this time, Kings and Queens are crowned upon this stone in Tara. The royal line of Solomon, through Zedekiah continues but they are now in the British Isles. Also, the Zarah branch of Judah is united with the royal branch of Solomon. This line is strengthened and continues on.

After about 500 AD, the stone of destiny was moved to Scotland. Fergus Mor McErc invaded the land of Scotland. He was of Irish descent but desired to be crowned King in Scotland, upon the stone of destiny.

"When the race of the Scots heard that the stone had this virtue (to roar), after Fergus the great, son of Earc, had obtained power of Scotland, and after he proposed to style himself King of Scotland, he sends information into the presence of his brother Muircheartach, son of Earc, of the race of Eiremhon, who was the King of Ireland at that time, to ask him to send him this stone, to sit upon, for the purposes of being proclaimed King of Scotland. Muircheartach sends the stone to him, and he is inaugurated King of Scotland on the same stone and he was the first King of Scotland of the Scottish nation."[18]

The stone of destiny remained with the Scots in Scotland until 1296 AD. At that time, Edward I of England took the stone to Westminster Abbey. There it remained for 700 years. All the Kings and Queens of England have been crowned upon this stone (except Mary). All of the royalty crowned upon this stone have been of the royal line of Judah.

"Comparatively few Bible scholars are aware of the fact that the Monarchy of Britain as well as most of the other monarchies of Europe are descended from Judah (recipient of the Sceptre promise-Gen. 49:10). In the Scottish National Library there is a Gaelic manuscript (by Dugald the Scot, son of McPhail in AD 1467) containing the complete genealogies of the Scottish Kings, showing their descent through the Irish Kings by way of Judah, Jacob, and Isaac back to Abraham. In Windsor Castle there is also a genealogical table showing the descent of the British Kings from David through the Irish and Scottish lines."[19]

In 1996, the stone of destiny was returned to Scotland.[20] Since this time, Scotland has started its own Parliament and Wales has started its own Assembly. With the move of this stone, these two countries may be instigating the first step in a series that will emancipate them from the sovereignty of England. This recent move of the stone may be the catalyst that sets off a chain reaction of events that lead to the end time events that culminate in the return of Jesus. Speaking of Jesus, could this stone be the same rock that Jesus built his church upon?

Many times in the New Testament Jesus alludes to a rock. Most theologians have taken this as an allegorical representation (as it is in one sense); that is not to be taken literally. It has been assumed that Jesus Christ is that rock, the foundation of the true church (as he is in one sense). I will devote the remainder of this chapter to the integration of the stone of destiny with the rock of Christ with the objective of ascertaining that they are the same rock. It is only after we have established this beyond a reasonable doubt that the entirety of the Bible can be drawn out to a logical conclusion, which includes the grand finale of the two witnesses. Let me begin with example one of the rock of Christ.

"Morever, brethren, I would not that ye should be ignorant, how that all our fathers were under the cloud, and all passed under the cloud, and all passed through the sea; And were all baptized into Moses in the cloud and in the sea: And did all eat the same spiritual meat; And did all drink the same spiritual drink: for they drank of that spiritual Rock that followed them: and that Rock was Christ."[21]

This verse is an excellent example tying the stone of destiny with Christ, the spiritual Rock. It has always been assumed that this rock was to typify Jesus. Let us imagine, for one moment, that the opposite is true. What if Jesus was to typify the rock? What if the church of Christ was to be built upon this rock? [22]

A good example to exemplify this is found in the book of Matthew. "He saith unto them, But whom say ye that I am? And Simon Peter answered and said, Thou art the Christ, the son of the living God. And Jesus answered and said unto him, Blessed art thou, Simon Bar-jona: for flesh and blood hath not revealed it unto thee, but my Father which is in heaven. And I say also unto thee, That thou art Peter, and upon this Rock I will build my church; And the gates of hell will not prevail against it."[23]

Take into account that Jesus spoke in parables. There were numerous reasons for this. At the time of Jesus, religious persecution was rampant. If Jesus had spoken plainly, all of his true followers would have been eliminated. So the church was shrouded in mystery. And the rock that Jesus' church was built upon was to remain an enigma. That is why many theologians debate whether that Rock was Jesus or Peter. Maybe that rock was neither. Maybe that rock was the anointed rock of Bethel.

Another example that pertains precisely to this theory is found in Ephesians. "Now therefore ye are no more strangers and foreigners, but fellow citizens with the saints, and of the household of God; And are built upon the foundation of the apostles and prophets, Jesus Christ himself being the chief corner stone; In whom all the building fitly framed together groweth into an holy temple in the Lord." [24]

Here we see Jesus portrayed as being the most important corner stone of the temple. What temple does this pertain to? Is this a spiritual or a physical temple? It could be in reference to both. It could also be in reference to the formation of God's end time church, which has not yet been built.

Isaiah portrays this "Therefore thus saith the Lord God, Behold, I lay in Zion for a foundation stone, a tried stone, a precious corner stone, a sure foundation: he that believeth shall not make haste."[25]

Keep in mind that this work is also about the two witnesses of Revelation. These two anointed ones are relevant to the building of God's temple in Jerusalem. Consider the stone of destiny in relationship to these two. If the stone moves back to Jerusalem, as it will, God's house will be re-established to its rightful city. One of these two witnesses will be coronated upon Jacob's Pillar, as the manner has always been, and the God of Abraham, Isaac, and Jacob will imbue God's end time church with power.

At the time of Jesus Christ, Peter was delegated as the chief apostle of the true church. This is stipulated in Matthew 17. This church was the very early church of Christ. What may not be known by many Bible scholars is that Peter spent a great deal of time in the British Isles. Recall that the stone of destiny arrived in Ireland in the year 584 BC. Although Jesus may not have known the exact location of the stone of Israel, he knew of its history and he knew of its existence. With the prophetic utterance of Jesus directed toward Peter, the prophecy of the rock was to be fulfilled. The Britons became the builders of the early church.[26]

Glastonbury is the site of the first Christian church outside of Jerusalem. It is located in southwest England approximately 125 miles west of London. According to tradition, the disciples of Christ built this church approximately 40 AD. Joseph of Arimathea, a disciple of Jesus, (he may have been his uncle as well), came here. This place (Glastonbury) was already, at this time, a Druid establishment of education. This is a subject in and of itself that this author does not have the time or the space to cover in this work. My purpose in mentioning this is to show a correlation between Peter, the early disciples of Jesus, the early church of Christ, and the stone of destiny.[27] This correlation continues between the early church, the stone of Israel, and the prophecy of Jesus.

"Jesus said unto them, Did ye never read in the scriptures, The stone which the builders rejected, the same is become the head of the corner: this is the Lord's doing, and it is marvelous in our eyes? Therefore say I unto you, The Kingdom of God shall be taken from you, and given to a nation bringing forth the fruits thereof. And whosoever shall fall on this stone shall be broken: but on whomsoever it shall fall, it will grind him to powder."[28]

"Therefore thus saith the Lord God, Behold, I lay in Zion for a foundation a stone, a tried stone, a precious corner stone, a sure foundation: he that believeth shall not make haste." [29]

What this demonstrates is that the early builders of the true church will reject that stone. Britain did that in late 1996. They handed over the stone of destiny to Scotland after 700 years of this stone being in their possession. Could this be the beginning of the formation of a new power that restores the stone to Jerusalem along with the people who go with it? God's end time believers will accomplish the building of the temple, in Jerusalem. The stone of destiny is destined to return with this end time power. This conclusion is certain.

"And in the days of these kings shall the God of heaven set up a kingdom, which shall never be destroyed: and the kingdom shall not be left to other people, but it shall break in pieces and consume all these kingdoms, and it shall stand forever. Forasmuch as thou sawest that the stone was cut out of the mountain without human hands, and that it brake in pieces the iron, the brass, the clay, the silver, and the gold; the great God hath made known what shall come to pass here after; and the dream is certain; and the interpretation thereof sure." [30]

In the next chapter, I will examine and clarify what kingdom this might be. With this relocation of the stone of destiny, momentous events are about to occur. This stone has changed hands, and God's end time power block is about to form.

Chapter Thirteen

The Coming Kingdom

A new power is inevitably forming from within the present chaos of this world.[1] It is destined: it is prophesied; it is unstoppable. Generally, it is assumed that this kingdom will arrive after Jesus returns. This is almost certainly not the scenario. Instead, this germinating, sovereign, supremacy is already in its genesis and will continue to grow until Jesus returns. Jesus will return just as the anti-Christ power is about to annihilate and decimate this supreme power into fragmentary pieces.[2] This disaster will be averted by the power of God, and the kingdom will stand forever. Daniel explicitly prophesies on his vision of this forming kingdom- "the stone kingdom".

"Thou, O King, sawest, and behold a great image, whose brightness was excellent, stood before thee; and the form thereof was terrible. This image's head was of fine gold, his breast and his arms of silver, his belly and his thighs of brass, His legs of iron, his feet part of iron and part of clay. Thou sawest til that a stone was cut out without hands, which smote the image upon his feet that were iron and clay, and brake them to pieces. Then was the iron, the clay, the brass, the silver, and the gold, broken to pieces together, and became like the chaff of the summer threshing floors; and the wind carried them away, that no place was found for them: and the stone that smote the image became a great mountain and filled the whole earth."[3]

Twice a certain stone is mentioned in Daniel 2. This stone is Christ. It is known by many names- the Bethel stone, the stone of Israel, the stone of destiny, the coronation stone. Whatever name one calls it, it is still Christ (or the anointed) pillar of Jacob. The power of God is intricately intertwined with this rock. The aforementioned stone kingdom has authorized power from the God of this universe due to the fact that this stone was anointed by Jacob, and a portion of his descendants were promised to God, as an offering from Jacob in exchange for protection and provisions to his descendants. Jacob made a covenant with God. And, God is an honorable creator. As I have already ascertained and explained to the best of my ability, this stone goes with Israel, or more appropriately Jacob. Jacob will stand for God and will not compromise their values or beliefs. Jacob is the coming kingdom that grows and smashes the 4th kingdom.[4]

This stone kingdom is made up of the "elect" of Israel.[5] I say elect because not all of Israel is destined to stand with this stone kingdom. Many will turn to the world system of belief and trust in their treasures and their money. The elect of Israel are of European descent- specifically the Scandinavian and British descended lineage. The Scandinavian and British countries will be the first to understand the implication of Bible prophecies that point directly at them. The stone of Israel now sits midway betwixt the Scandinavian countries and Britain. It is in Scotland for safekeeping. Once this prophesied power begins to snowball, there will be no stopping it. It will continue to expand until it covers much of the world. This is when everyone will be required to make a choice that will affect every single person's eternal destiny. The question will be... Do you choose to follow Christ or the anti-Christ?[6]

The fourth kingdom is here. It is surreptitiously expanding economically, politically, and religiously. This fourth kingdom will be put in check by the "stone" kingdom that forms from within the chaos and turmoil of this New World order- the fourth kingdom. Daniel foretold of this fourth kingdom...

"And this fourth kingdom shall be strong as iron: forasmuch as iron breaketh in pieces and subdueth all things: and as iron that breaketh all these, shall it break in pieces and bruise. And whereas thou sawest the feet and toes, part of potters clay and part of iron, the kingdom shall be divided: but there shall be in it of the strength of the iron mixed with miry clay. And as the toes of the feet were part of iron, and part of clay, so the kingdom shall be partly strong, and partly broken. And whereas thou sawest iron mixed with miry clay, they shall mingle themselves with the seed of men: but they shall not cleave one to another, even as iron is not mixed with clay. And in the days of these kings shall the God of heaven set up a kingdom, which shall never be destroyed: and the kingdom will not be left to other people, but it shall break in pieces and consume all these kingdoms, and it shall stand forever. Forasmuch as thou sawest that the stone was cut out of the mountain without hands, and that it break in pieces the iron, the brass, the clay, the silver, and the gold; the great God hath made known to the king what shall come to pass hereafter: and the dream is certain, and the interpretation thereof sure."[7]

Yes, the fourth kingdom is here! The European Monetary Union was consolidated on January 1, 1999. A single currency has been selected –the Euro. The Euro zone is now in place and includes 11 countries. The countries of the Euro zone include…Austria, Belgium, Finland, France, Germany, Ireland, Italy, Luxembourg, Netherlands, Portugal and Spain. This Euro zone will expand in the near future. The EMU is an economic alliance, as the name implies, as well as a political entity. A central bank has already been set up for this Euro zone. It is located in Frankfurt, Germany, and will have complete autonomy, independent of all political authority. This bank will exert control over the interest rates of the whole European union. In other words, Germany will rule! This revived "Roman" empire will revolve around German control of the economic and political scene.

Where does the United States of America fit into this emerging picture? The answers may surprise and shock you. In 1995, the New Transatlantic Agenda was signed. This treaty focuses on consolidating the EMU with the United States as far as trade, economic, and political issues are concerned. The United States is increasingly becoming an auxiliary entity of the EMU. The US turns to the European Union in partnership regarding issues of world leadership. The New Transatlantic Agenda sees frequent consultations between United states leaders and European union leaders on issues ranging from democracy, foreign policy, global challenges, peace treaties, and humanitarian aid. Yes, the United States of America (not all of its residents) is destined to become a part of the 4th kingdom of Bible prophecy.[8]

Have you ever heard of Norden? Norden includes the Nordic regions of Norway, Sweden, Iceland, the Aland Islands, Denmark, Greenland, and Finland. Norden is not a Federal state. In many ways, it is a single entity. This is an area of the world where neighbors watch over neighbors. The Nordic people practice democracy in action rather than just in speech. This is called Nordic cooperation. And, it is expanding. These countries cooperate in many areas including civil rights, culture, education, environment, economy, fisheries, legal issues, and research. They support one another as a single people before they practice capitalistic ethics. This is the Scandinavian way! This is the strength of Jacob. These countries are destined to become leading players in the "stone" kingdom. It is interesting to note that Norway has opted to stay out of any European integration over the years. It is also interesting to note that Denmark and Sweden have decided against joining the Euro, for now. Britain has also declined the invitation.[9]

Since Great Britain has declined to become a part of the EMU, at least for now, what will become of it? Bill Jamieson, Economics Editor of the Sunday Telegraph, in his article, "Britains Global Future," has this to say… " We have developed a far better system of accountable government than most continental nations. We have, to date, shown more concern for the democratic rights of our citizens than many regimes of Continental Europe. We have invested far more than they in properly provisioning for our own pensions in retirement. Other nations may pay out pensions on a larger scale but they have to fund them through increased borrowing. Continental taxation is likely to rise sharply. Inside EMU, as taxes are harmonised, British workers will have to contribute much more." Bill Jamieson continues... "Enough is enough. We have not enjoyed this experiment in pooled sovereignty for the past 25 years, and now, give notice that we wish to end it."[10]

From The Spectator, February 5, 2000, edition... "Just when you thought it was safe," Andrew Marr has this to say, "There is an air of triumph in the camp of euro sceptics. Its crash below dollar parity; the stain of corruption across French and German politics; the feeble toots, of the pro-euro politicians; the Treasury's clear reluctance about monetary union; the latest polling, showing a massive majority against the euro and a hefty 34 percent wanting out of the EU altogether; Wim Duisenberg's remark about Britain being ready to join the currency block. They have given the impression that the battle is virtually over. Wan faced, many pro-Europeans have concluded the same. It is all a little like that story from the early afternoon of June 1815 when an ebullient Napoleon is said to have ordered messengers to Paris announcing his triumph over the allied forces led so pathetically by Wellington. The Scots Greys are a writhing mound of lancers' pin-cushions, the red lines are wavering, the groan of the Guards rends the smoky sky. They may have lost an election but the euro-sceptics have won the fight that really matters. Not quite, my friends. Not yet."[11]

What will become of Britain?[12] The truth of the matter is that Britain is in a delicately precarious situation, both politically and economically. Global economic downturns could force Britain to integrate into the EMU. Britain lies between a rock and a hard place. It is difficult to say what will occur in the not to distant future. According to Andrew Marr, "The euro argument has been characterised by two lies: the pro-euro lie is that there can be monetary union and a larger EU without further integration. There cannot be. The entire mechanism would seize up, then break up. The anti-euro lie is that Britain has a secure future in the world outside the eurozone. Nothing scares ministers more than the thought of Washington's indifference and an EU shaped and driven without a thought for London."13

If Great Britain joins the EMU, what will become of its people? If Britain vows to stay out, what will become of its people? It appears that Britain is in a catch22. But, wait. Never underestimate the power of God.

"Morever, thou son of man, take thee one stick, and write upon it, For Judah, and for the Children of Israel his companions: then take another stick, and write upon it, For Joseph, the stick of Ephraim, and for all the house of Israel his companions: And join them one to another into one stick: and they shall become one in thine hand. And when the children of thy people shall speak unto thee, saying, Wilt thou not show us what thou meanest by these? Say unto them, Thus saith the Lord God; Behold, I will take the stick of Joseph, which is in the hand of Ephraim, and the tribes of Israel his fellows, and will put them with him, even with the stick of Judah, and make them one stick, and they shall be one in mine hand. And the sticks whereon thou writest shall be in thine hand before their eyes. And say unto them, Thus saith the Lord God; Behold, I will take the children of Israel from among the heathen, whither they be gone, and will gather them on every side, and bring them into their own land: And I will make them one nation in the land upon the mountains of Israel." 14

Britain's dissidents are bound to an everlasting covenant. They will be forced home to Jerusalem and be joined together with the house of Judah. The Bible explicitly details this. What initiates this destined reunion is not stated but; it is certain to occur. Perhaps God will place these people in a situation similar to what I have just previously written about, where they have no alternative but to leave. This could explain a scenario where the EMU is forced upon these people-giving them no other way out. God does work in mysterious ways! Jerusalem cannot house everyone. Where else might they go?

Scandinavia may serve as a place of refuge for some of these displaced people. Scandinavia could contain more people if a desperate situation called for it. During the tyranny of Hitler, when he went on his Jew killing frenzy, Denmark took a strong position to see that many Jews made it safely to an area of Sweden where they were safe. This was done with great risk to their own lives. Scandinavia has always helped those in need because they try to emulate the ways of Jesus. In the coming redemption process, they will stand.

Although it is not entirely clear, at this point, as to where all these Israelites will assimilate, it is becoming increasingly obvious that the Scandinavian countries (Dan), Britain (Ephraim), N. Ireland, Scotland, and Wales (Ephraim and Dan), will league together in some sort of alliance as this stone kingdom forms. It is in the gestation stage right now and will grow explosively right before the return of Jesus. This allegiance is destined to stand behind the house of Judah in Jerusalem, also.

When the two witnesses come on the scene of world history, many of Dan and Ephraim from around the world will recognize who they are and turn to God with a truly contrite heart. They will also support the stone kingdom- which is anointed. Many others of Dan and Particularly Ephraim will not support this kingdom and shall be condemned along with all the powerful forces of the anti-Christ. Have you never wondered why Dan and Ephraim are not sealed in the book of Revelation? They are not sealed because they are either chosen or destroyed! This brings us to the topic of the redemption.

There are 144,000 sealed from all the tribes of Israel in the book of Revelation. Where are Dan and Ephraim? They are conspicuously absent from the sealing. Consider, for a moment, after all the evidence, where Dan and Ephraim converge. They converge in the British Isles and the Scandinavian countries. This is Jacob, and most will be redeemed during the time of Jacob's trouble.

The redemption begins with two things. The first definitive sign of redemption is that the gospel of the kingdom will be published worldwide. Obviously, the truth about the kingdom of Christ has not yet been published or the end would already be here. This is prophesied in Matthew 24:14. The second sign that ushers in this redemption and restoration is the appearance of the last Elijah. This Elijah will decipher and proclaim this endtime gospel.

Bobby Rich, author of "The Last Prophet," has this to say concerning Elijah... "As the scrolls describe the final symbolic "Elijah" prophet we see the same opposition to his message, especially among the seekers after smooth things, who prefer their own mental delusions – to the vision the prophet carries as given to him by God. As with Elijah this final prophet will also be forced into exile from his land and be hunted by those who wish to kill him."[15]

So here we have a synopsis of the final "stone" kingdom that arises in the last days. The gospel of the kingdom must be published, worldwide, first. Elijah is the delegated instrument to accomplish that task. A faithful remnant of Ephraim (British Isles) and some of its descent and Dan (Scandinavian lineage worldwide, and Wales, Scotland, and N. Ireland) start emigrating to Jerusalem as well as to Scandinavia after the Coming Elijah is exiled to Jerusalem. Then, the stone of Israel returns to Jerusalem as the cornerstone for the third temple. This is the beginning of the redemption of God.

"Behold, I will bring them from the north country, and gather them from the coasts of the earth, and with them the blind and the lame, the woman with child and her that travaileth with child together: a great company shall return thither. They shall come with weeping, and with supplications will I lead them: I will cause them to walk by the rivers of waters in a straight way, wherein they shall not stumble; for I am a father to Israel, and Ephraim is my firstborn. Hear the word of the Lord,

O ye nations, and declare it in the isles a far off, and say, He that scattereth Israel, will gather him, and keep him, as a shepherd does his flock."[16]

Chapter Fourteen

The Elijah to Come

"Behold, I will send you Elijah the prophet before the coming of the great and dreadful day of the Lord: And he shall turn the heart of the fathers to the children, and the heart of the children to their fathers, lest I come and smite the earth with a curse."[1]

Elijah is to return. This is not referring to a literal return of Elijah the Tishbite. This is in reference to one who comes in the power and the spirit of Elijah to herald in the coming of the Lord. This Elijah will prepare the way and show the elect of Israel the true path of righteousness.[2]

The first Elijah came on the scene during a time of great apostasy of the Israelites. He is described as Elijah the Tishbite, an inhabitant of Gilead. He is mentioned in the book of Kings. Nothing is written in regards to his lineage, or if he was an Israelite at all. All that is known is that he comes with the power of God to warn the Israelites of the consequence of their willful disregard for the Laws of God.

"And Elijah the Tishbite, who was of the inhabitants of Gilead, said unto Ahab, As the Lord God of Israel liveth, before whom I stand, there shall not be dew nor rain these years, but according to my word."[3]

Elijah is instructed to go to King Ahab and tell him to repent and turn from heathen practices. The house of Israel during this time (874-854 BC) was not following the ways of God. Because of this, judgement began to fall. Elijah was the chosen instrument to implement that judgement from God. The Israelites did not want to turn from their wickedness so Elijah requested that God show his power to the people.

"Hear me, O Lord, hear me, that this people may know that thou art the Lord God, and that thou hast turned their heart back again. Then the fire of the Lord fell, and consumed the burnt sacrifice, and the wood, and the stones, and the dust, and licked up the water that was in the trench. And when all the people saw it, they fell on their faces: and they said, The Lord, he is the God; the Lord, he is the God."4

God empowered the first Elijah with authority to judge the wicked and turn the righteous back to a repentant heart. His authority was awesome. He stopped the rain for three and one half years. He created food when there was none He brought a dead child back to life.

The second Elijah came to prepare the way for Jesus, the Messiah. He was also selected by God to turn the people to repentance in preparation for the Kingdom of God. This is what Jesus had to say in regards to John the Baptist...

"And as they departed, Jesus began to say unto the multitudes concerning John, What went ye out in the wilderness to see? A reed shaken with the wind? But went ye out for to see? A prophet? yea, I say unto you, and more than a prophet. For this is he, of whom it is written, Behold, I send my messenger before thy face which shall prepare thy way before thee."5

The third and final Elijah comes to restore all things. First, he comes to call the house of Judah and the house of Israel to repentance. The house of Judah is admonished for rejecting Jesus as Lord and savior. The house of Israel is admonished for disregarding the Laws of God and treating the death of Jesus as a small thing. Then, he comes to call the "house of David" home to Jerusalem to begin the restoration of the Davidic temple in Jerusalem. He also comes to find the solution to the, thus far, irreconcilable differences between the Jews and the true Christians. His message will be heard primarily by the modern day Mannasah branch of the house of Israel (USA), and the countries of

Canada, Australia, and New Zealand, as well as the state of Israel and the North and Northwestern European countries (Norway, Sweden, Denmark, Finland, the Netherlands, Northern Ireland, Wales, Scotland, and England).

What does the Bible tell us about this coming prophet? In Ezekiel 2 and in Revelation 10 someone is given a scroll to eat. This scroll contains writing with words of woe and mourning. Let's take a look at these two Biblical books beginning with Ezekiel.

"And he said unto me, Son of man, I send thee to the children of Israel, to a rebellious nation that hath rebelled against me: they and their fathers have transgressed against me, even unto this very day. And thou shalt speak my words unto them, whether they will hear, or whether they will forbear: for they are most rebellious. But thou, son of man, hear what I say unto thee; Be not thou rebellious like that rebellious house; open thy mouth, and eat that I give thee. And when I looked, behold, an hand was sent unto me; and, lo, a roll of a book was therein; And he spread it before me; and it was written within and without: and there was written lamentations, and mourning and woe."[6]

"But thou, O Daniel, shut up the words and seal the book, even to the time of the end: many shall run to and fro, and knowledge shall be increased."[7]

Let's proceed to Revelation 10. This is the revelation of John. "and he had in his hand a little book open; and he set his right foot upon the sea, and his left foot on the earth. And cried with a loud voice, as when a lion roareth and when he had cried, seven thunders uttered their voices. And when the seven thunders had uttered their voices, I was about to write: and I heard a voice from heaven saying unto me, seal up those things which the seven thunders uttered, and write them not."[8]

We see here that John was forbidden to reveal what the scrolls said. It is not until immediately proceeding the arrival of the two witnesses that the prophecy is unsealed. Who do you suppose will unlock end time prophecy? Would not the last Elijah be the most likely candidate? The

Elijah to come will be the one to interpret the sealed prophecy. God gives this prophet complete comprehension of the Bible and its interpretation.[9]

I have just outlined a general description of the office of Elijah from Biblical scripture. The first Elijah came at a time in history when the house of Judah was a separate kingdom from the house of Israel. John the Baptist, the second Elijah, came at another time in history when the two houses were divided and the Israelites were scattered and lost. The third Elijah comes on the scene of world history at a time when the two houses of Israel (Judah and Ephraim) are separate, to unite them into one kingdom. This period is fast approaching. Elijah will come on the scene when nations are in turmoil and the countries of Jacob are in danger of being placed under the power of a tyrannical dictatorship. Is not this time now?

What do different authoritative sources have to say about this coming prophet? I have put together a collection of citations from several different sources in connection with this topic. They all seem to come together into one general theme. Let me begin with Yair Davidy who approaches this from a Jewish perspective.

According to Yair Davidy, world recognized authority in the field of lost Israelite identity, the order of redemption proceeds with the appearance of the Messiah, son of Joseph, followed by the arrival of the second Messiah, son of David. Before this occurs, somebody representing Elijah will appear. "Behold I will send you Elijah the prophet before the coming of the great and dreadful day of the Lord." And he shall turn the heart of the fathers to the children, and the heart of the children to their father, lest I come and smite the earth with a curse" (Malachi 4: 5-6).

"A definition of the aspect of Elijah is the complete clarification of the truth..[as Elijah said:] How long halt ye between two opinions?" (I Kings 18;21) .[10]

I will continue on with sources from Bobby Rich, author of the Last Prophet. At the time of the end someone known as the teacher of righteousness will appear. This teacher of righteousness, also known as the final prophet, will appear to the world as the interpreter of the Bible. This prophet will receive inspiration and direction from God. There is a delay mentioned in the Bible in connection with this last prophet's message. When this prophet goes public, the delay will be over. This last prophet, teacher of righteousness, is the Elijah who comes to prepare the way for the Lord .[11]

There will be opposition to this coming prophet's message, particularly by those who seek the easy road and do not wish to face reality. Because of all this opposition, this person will be forced into exile from his home. Many will seek to harm this person because they do not wish to believe the message given to him by God. Some people will understand and listen to the message of this prophet, and this will distinguish between the righteous and the wicked.

This last Elijah "appears to be a MAN OF CALAMITIES, of stumbling rather than success. This prophet is a man betrayed by those who eat his bread and maligned in gossip with a resultant loss of reputation, ridiculed and scorned, beset by serious illnesses, financially unsuccessful, a victim of schemers, being scourged by God for unknown reasons. He has visited the gates of death and commonly experiences pain on an ongoing basis. This person is considered a broken vessel beset by bad health and serious personal problems with a variety of trials. However as time advances a different aspect will emerge because at some point God will begin to establish and lift up this prophet, and the prophet's situation makes a dramatic change. The scrolls also make it clear that God will not allow this prophet to be put down by others forever because in due time God himself will strengthen the prophet and the mysteries he holds will no longer be hidden."[12]

The book of Habakkuk gives a description of the vision from this prophet. " I will stand upon my watch, and set me upon the tower, and will watch to see what he will say unto me, and what I shall answer when I am reproved. And the Lord answered me, and said, Write the vision, and make it plain upon tables that he may run that readeth it.

For the vision is yet for an appointed time, but at the end it will speak, and not lie: thou it tarry, wait for it; because it will surely come, it will not tarry." [13]

Bobby Rich has compiled a list of descriptive characteristics of this prophet from his book. I am going to list them. "Dim eyesight from waiting. Poor health, pain, chronic loss of strength- heart fails. My soul has journeyed to the gates of death- God has not placed my support in gain- no fleshly refuge. All who have eaten my bread have lifted their heel against me. Opponents hate and wrongfully render evil for good. Object of a treacherous tongue. Those who do not esteem me hate and despise me. My enemies hate, speak evil and devise my hurt- seeking my life. Psalms 42 states that he used to go with a multitude that kept a pilgrim feast. This may imply he once kept the seven Levitical Old Testament Holy days but no longer does. Psalms 40:3 states this prophet will compose a new song which many will see and believe. Those who listen to him and believe are called "of my council or of my covenant." [14]

From the Dead Sea Scrolls Translated by Professor Dr. Florentino García Martínez, Director of the Qumran Institute at Groningen, the Netherlands, I have quoted fragments that may pertain to this last Elijah "1. I remain silent […] 2.[…] my arm is broken at the elbow, my feet sink in the mud, my eyes are blind from having seen evil, 3. my ears, through hearing the shedding of blood, my heart is horrified at wicked schemes, for Belial is present when the inclination of their being becomes apparent. 4. The foundations of my building have crumbled, my bones have been disjointed, my entrails heave like a boat in the rage of the storm 5. my heart pulsates to destruction, a whirlwind overwhelms me, due to wickedness of their sin." [15]

So far I have provided several reliable and authoritative sources that provide an insight into possible characteristics of this Elijah. They all seem to point to a person who has faced many, beyond and above the normal, trials. The portrait painted shows a person who has survived numerous ordeals, betrayals, and injustices at the hands of others.

Through it all, this person has not lost faith in God, and continues to praise his holiness. It is through all these trials that this person grows strong and comes to power as God's last Elijah. I will continue now and link this Elijah to his last human mission, that as one of the two witnesses, and the priestly Messiah to come.

According to Professor Dr. Florentino García Martínez, Director of the Qumran Institute, in Groningen, the Netherlands, there are numerous fragments from the Dead Sea scrolls that point to two messiahs. Some, specifically, point to an Elijah figure. "It seems more difficult to determine who this "Interpreter of the Law" is. Two interpretations have been suggested. Starcky identified him with the expected eschatological prophet although this identification starts from a false premise, the non separation of the two "Messiahs" of Aaron and Israel in CD. The more prevalent opinion, following Van der Woude identifies this "Interpreter of the Law" with the "Messiah of Aaron." I.e. the "priest Messiah" who should be identified with the eschatological figure of Elijah. Van der Woude's reasoning essentially is as follows. The "Interpreter of the Law" of this passage is a person from the future and thus distinct from the "Interpreter of the Law" who occurs in CD V17 and is a person from the past. This person is found in parallel with the "Prince of the whole Congregation," who is a messianic figure identical with the "Messiah of Israel." [16]

There is reference to these same two Messiahs in Numbers. "I shall see him, but not now: I shall behold him, but not nigh: there shall come a star out of Jacob, and a sceptre shall rise out of Israel, and shall smite the corners of Moab, and destroy all the children of Sheth. And Edom shall be a possession for his enemies; and Israel shall do valiantly. Out of Jacob shall come he that shall have dominion, and shall destroy him that remaineth of the city." [17]

Here this Messiah of Aaron is identified as a star out of Jacob. This adds dimension to this priestly Messiah, the Elijah to Come. As Jacob is identified, in a previous chapter, "House of David" as associated primarily with the Scandinavian countries, as well as the Netherlands, Scotland, Wales, and Northern Ireland. This priestly Messiah must then be an ancestral descendant (not necessarily born there) from at least one of these countries in contrast to Britain proper (England) which is specifically connected with Israel. So, now we see that the Elijah to come has the bloodline of Levi and Nathan (Judah) and is a descendant of at least one of the fore-mentioned countries.

In my next chapter, I will deal with the two witnesses of the Apocalypse. Their identities can now be realized through my in depth research. I will point out specific references to these two messengers that identify them. These references are scattered throughout the Bible. When this work is complete, a genealogical lineage will be established for both people. Their ancestral lines are mentioned in many different places, and are mixed. The sex of one of these two may take people by complete surprise. But remember, the Bible was written by the inspiration of many different prophets. These prophecies must all be fulfilled. That is why such a strong admonition is given in the book of Revelation against adding or taking away from the Holy Bible.

Chapter Fifteen

Two Witnesses or Two Messiahs?

Two witnesses are mentioned only in the book of Revelation.[1] There is very little stated about them directly; so they are obscure individuals who have an extremely important end-time mission. Many "Christians" have explanations pertaining to these two that do not serve them justice. Neither do these explanations give them honor that is due. Sometimes, the two witnesses are glossed over as not important to an overall interpretation of the Bible. But, two witnesses are mentioned at the end of the Bible. If we cannot understand the ending, we did not understand the book. Who are these two? How can we best explain their presence and their significance? Two "anointed" rulers are mentioned throughout the Bible.[2] There are many specific references to these two in the Old Testament. There are some references to them in the New Testament. The New Testament references are more elusive and obscure than are those that are found in the Old Testament. Jesus pointed to these two in his aphorisms. He did not come right out and say anything clear regarding them; but they are mentioned. Let me begin with Biblical examples from the Old Testament that point the way.

Example one is found in the book of Numbers. "And now, behold, I go unto my people: come therefore, and I will advertise thee what this people shall do to thy people in the latter days. And he took up his parable, and said, Balaam the son of Beor hath said, and the man whose eyes are open hath said: He hath said, which heard the words of God, and knew the knowledge of the most High, which saw the vision of the Almighty, falling into a trance, but having his eyes open: I shall see him, but not now: I shall behold him, but not nigh: there shall come a star out of Jacob, and a sceptre shall rise out of Israel, and shall smite the corners of Moab, and destroy all the children of Sheth. And Edom shall be a possession, Seir also shall be a possession for his enemies; and Israel shall do valiantly. Out of Jacob shall come he that shall have dominion, and shall destroy him that remaineth of the city." [3]

Here is reference to the latter days and to the two anointed ones. One of these is out of Jacob. The other one is out of Israel. Here we see a differentiation is made between Jacob and Israel. A star out of Jacob is the one who is to have dominion. This would be an identifying mark of the priest Messiah who is also a Star of David. The sceptre out of Israel is the Prince of Davidic lineage from the line of Zerubbabel.

Example two is found in Isaiah. "Nevertheless the dimness shall not be such as was in her vexation, when at first he lightly afflicted the land of Zebulun and the land of Naphtali, and afterward did more grievously afflict her by way of the sea, beyond Jordon, in Galilee of the nations. The people that walked in darkness have seen a great light: they that dwell in the land of the shadow of death, upon them hath the light shined. Thou hast multiplied the nation, and not increased the joy: they joy before thee according to the joy in harvest, and as men rejoice when they divide the spoil. For thou hast broken the yoke of his burden, and the staff of his shoulder, the rod of his oppressor, as in the day of Midian. For every battle of the warrior is with confused noise, and garments rolled in blood; but this shall be with burning and fuel of fire. For unto us a child is born, unto us a son is given: and the government shall be upon his shoulder:" [4]

At first reading this may appear to refer to Jesus; as it does. But there is also reference to the two other anointed figures. Jesus alludes to this same passage in the New Testament and shows that he comes to fulfill the part. Jesus is the chief Messiah. In this passage reference is made to Naphtali and to Zebulun. If you recall, Yair Davidy associates Naphtali with Norway and Zebulun with the Netherlands. This is clearly pertinent to two other anointed rulers; one is a descendant of Norwegian lineage. The other is a descendant of Dutch blood.[5]

According to Yair Davidy, world recognized authority in the field of lost Israelite identity, Naphtali is identified with Norway. "It is hereby proposed that the earlier NAPHTALITES and the bulk of the Naphtalite nation who went westward and were since unheard of became the Vikings of Scandinavia, especially of Norway. Scandinavia in the 500's and 500's c.e received an influx of settlers from the east. This was shortly after the bulk of Naphtalites had embarked on their westward trek." [6]

"The Netherlands (Holland) features lions on the Coat of Arms. Lions symbolise all of Israel especially as united under the house of David from Judah whose especial sign is a lion. Similarly, Zebulon, though dominant in Holland, is also represented by "Halland" of the Southwest Coast of Sweden, and by hallin in Norway which names come from that of Elon, son of Zebulon, as does the name for Holland itself."[7]

A third example, from the Old Testament, that points to two anointed rulers is found in Jeremiah. "Behold, the days come, Saith the LORD, that I will perform that good thing which I have promised unto the house of Israel and to the house of Judah. In those days, and at that time, will I cause the branch of righteousness to grow up unto David; and he shall execute judgement and righteousness in the land. In those days shall Judah be saved, and Jerusalem shall dwell safely: and this is the name wherewith she shall be called, The LORD our righteousness. For thus saith the LORD; David shall never want a man to sit upon the throne of the house of Israel; Neither shall the priests the Levites want a man before me to offer burnt offerings, and to kindle meat offerings, and to do sacrifice continually."[8]

Whether this was added from original Greek is insignificant since the Authorized King James Version of the Bible is the inspired Version. This is due to the fact that the stone of destiny was in England at the time of the writing. The word becomes prophecy.

This passage refers to two anointed rulers who will rule from Jerusalem at the end of days. The branch of David is the Prince of the Congregation, the Sceptre of Israel. The other figure is the Priestly Messiah and she shall be called the LORD our righteousness. Yes, this appears to be a woman. This person is the star out of Jacob who is of Norwegian descent, and a descendant of Nathan. She is also of the tribe of Levi, probably Zadok.[9]

Example four can be found in Zechariah. This book expounds on the identity of these two anointed figures. "And he showed me Joshua the high priest standing before the angel of the lord, and Satan standing at his right hand to resist him. And the Lord said unto Satan, The Lord rebuke thee, O Satan; even the LORD that hath chosen Jerusalem rebuke thee: is not this a brand plucked from the fire? Now Joshua was clothed with filthy garments, and stood before the angel. And he answered and spake unto those that stood before him, saying, Take away the filthy garments from him. And unto him he said, Behold, I have caused thine iniquity to pass from thee, and I will clothe thee with change of raiment. And I said, Let them set a fair mitre upon his head, and clothed him with garments. And the angel of the Lord stood by. And the angel of the LORD protested unto Joshua, saying, Thus saith the LORD of hosts, if thou wilt walk in my ways, and if thou wilt keep my charge, then thou shalt also judge my house, and shalt also keep my courts, and I will give thee places to walk among these that stand by. Hear now, O Joshua the high priest, thou, and thy fellows that sit before thee: for they are men wondered at: for behold, I will bring forth my servant the BRANCH. For behold the stone that I have laid before

Joshua; upon one stone shall be seven eyes; behold, I will engrave the graving thereof, saith the LORD of hosts, and I will remove the iniquity of that land in one day." [10]

Wow! This really adds substance. Joshua, the high priest, is crowned in Jerusalem next to the stone of Israel. Joshua is a symbolic name. From the book of Jeremiah I have already ascertained that this person is probably a woman, a Levite priest, that sits upon the throne of David who is also of the house and lineage of David through Nathan. There is also a possibility that this person descends from a royal lineage of Solomon.

"And the angel that talked with me came again, and waked me, as a man that is wakened out of his sleep, And said unto me, what seest thou? And I said, I have looked, and behold a candlestick all of gold, with a bowl upon the top of it, and his seven lamps thereon, and seven pipes to the seven lamps, which are upon the top thereof: And two olive trees by it, one upon the right side of the bowl, and the other upon the left side thereof. So I answered and spake to the angel that talked with me, saying, What are these, my lord? Then the angel that talked with me answered and said unto me, Knowest thou not what these be? And I said, No, my lord. Then he answered and spake unto me saying, This is the word of the Lord unto Zerubbabel, saying, Not by might, nor by power, but by my spirit, saith the LORD of hosts. Who art thou, O great mountain? before Zerubbabel thou shalt become a plain: and he shall bring forth the headstone thereof with shoutings, crying, Grace, grace unto it. Morever the word of the LORD came unto me, saying, The hands of Zerubbabel have laid the foundation of this house; his hands shall also finish it; and thou shalt know that the LORD of hosts hath sent me unto you. For who hath despised the day of small things? for they shall rejoice, and shall see the plummet in the hand of Zerubbabel with those seven; they are the eyes of the LORD, which run to and fro through the whole earth. Then answered I, and said unto him, What be these two olive branches which through the two golden pipes empty the golden oil out of themselves? And he answered me and said, Knowest thou not what these be? And I said, No, my lord. Then said he, These are the two anointed ones that stand by the LORD of the whole earth." [11]

Here we have an entire chapter devoted to these two anointed ones. Notice that they are called olive trees. Two olive trees are also mentioned in the book of Revelation where the two witnesses are mentioned. This is evidence that ties these two anointed ones with the two witnesses. Zechariah and Revelation are referring to the exact same two people. These two are the ones that stand by the Lord of the earth. They are the chosen two who stand by Jesus, one on his left side, the other on his right side, in his coming kingdom.

Zerubbabel is the coming Prince of the Congregation. He is a descendant of Jeconias the cursed King. This is why he is not crowned King in Jerusalem. Instead, Joshua, the high priest is crowned. It is a duel messianic rule.[12] Let me recapitulate.

"Is this man Coniah a despised broken idol? is he a vessel wherein is no pleasure? wherefore are they cast out, he and his seed, and are cast into a land which they know not? Thus saith the LORD, write ye this man childless, a man that shall not prosper in his days: for no man of his seed shall prosper, sitting upon the throne of David, and ruling any more in Judah." [13]

Zerubbabel is the Sceptre of Israel. He will rule from Jerusalem with the other anointed figure, Joshua the high priest. Zerubbabel will have tremendous power but the Levite priest, the star out of Jacob, will have the dominion. This is a dual partnership that must occur in order for Bible prophecy to be completely fulfilled. This time is near.[14]

I will continue on into New Testament analysis of prophecies concerning these two anointed leaders. The New Testament does not clarify the existence of these two very specifically. There is more allusion to these two than there is actual reference to them. There is reason for this. You must consider the time in history and the parables that Jesus spoke. The truth was not meant to be completely revealed at that time. The truth is meant to be revealed now! The full truth of the gospel of the kingdom is to be unsealed right before the day of the Lord!

The first allusion to two Messiahs in the New Testament can be found in Matthew and Luke. This is where we find two conflicting genealogies of Jesus Christ. There has been much confusion over these genealogies since Jesus was supposed to have born from a virgin birth. In Matthew, the lineage comes through Jeconias- eventually through Zorobabel, and then through Jacob who sired Joseph, the husband of Mary. Mary is the mother of Christ. In Luke we see a different picture. Luke actually mentions different tribes of Israel, repetitively. Look closely. First, we see this genealogy is of David through his son Nathan. The name Joseph (tribe?) is mentioned four times. The name Levi (tribe?) is mentioned twice. The name Simeon (tribe?) is mentioned once. The name Judah (tribe?) is mentioned three times. The terminology that is also repeated is, for example, "Which was the son of Melea, which was the son of Menan, which was the son of Mattatha, which was the son of Nathan, which was the son of David." [15] The point I am trying to make is, these are all sons of God, which come from Nathan. From the discrepancies in these two genealogies, I have come to the conclusion that the two witnesses, as two anointed Messiahs, come from these lineages, one from each.

A second allusion to two Messiahs is found in Mark. "They said unto him, Grant unto us that we may sit, one on thy right hand, and the other on thy left hand, in thy glory. But Jesus said unto them, Ye know not what ye ask; can ye drink of the cup that I drink of? and be baptized with the baptism that I am baptized with? And they said unto him, We can. And Jesus said unto them, Ye shall indeed drink of the cup that I drink of; and with the baptism that I am baptized withal shall ye be baptized; But to sit on my right hand and on my left hand is not mine to give; but IT SHALL BE GIVEN TO THEM for whom it is prepared." [16]

Take a look at Zechariah 4.[17] Here it mentions two anointed servants that stand by the Lord of the earth. Could these two be the two witnesses of Jesus that are given the privilege of sitting next to Jesus in his coming kingdom?

Let me take you, now, to some Dead Sea Scroll material and see what is said in regards to messianic prophecy. The Dead Sea Scrolls contain a wealth of information pertaining to two Messiahs within an apocalyptic theme. There is much information that points to more than one Messiah. After taking the Dead Sea Scroll information into account, the overall meaning of the Bible takes on a different tone. And that tone involves end-time decisions that are much more complicated than whether one has accepted Jesus as their Savior. Although the decision to accept Jesus as Savior is paramount to salvation, there is one more decision that will have to be made by everyone. That decision is the answer to two questions... Do you choose to follow God and the path of right-eousness? Or do you chose to claim Christ while you are at the same time traveling down the road to ultimate destruction? That choice is yours.

From Messianic Hopes in the Qumran Writings there are references to two Messiahs. I will quote some of this information authored by Professor Dr. Florentino García Martínez who heads the Qumran Institute at the University of Groningen, the Netherlands. Then I will expound on this information within the context of this chapter. Example one from Professor Florentino García Martínez' research and writing is as follows...

"Perhaps the most studied and best known element of Qumran Messianism is its two-headed messianism: the hope in a double "Messiah," "the Messiah of Aaron" and "theMessiah of Israel." The key text comes from the Rule of the Community.

1QSIX9-11

9 They should not depart from any counsel of the law in order to walk 10 in complete stubborness of their heart, but instead shall be ruled by the first directives which the men of the community began to

be taught11 until the prophet comes, and the Messiahs of Aaron and Israel. blank (DSST, 13-14).

The text is crystal clear and expresses without any doubt the hope, within the Qumran community, in the future coming of the two "anointed ones" (in the plural). The "Messiah of Aaron" and the "Messiah of Israel," two figures who apparently correspond to the "priestly Messiah" and the "royal Messiah" whom we came across as separate figures in the proceeding texts. It tells us nothing about their functions, about the biblical basis which allowed their hope to develop, their possible identification with other titles used in the texts to give these figures a name. The exception is the priestly character implied in the provenance "from Aaron" of one of them and of the non-priestly character of the other who comes "from Israel." In spite of its laconic nature, this text is fundamental since it allows us to clarify a whole series of expressions which mention the "anointed one" (in the singular) of Aaron and of Israel as referring not to a single "Messiah," priest and king at the same time, but to two "Messiahs": a "Messiah-priest" and a "lay Messiah." [18]

Here we see two Messiahs. There is the Messiah of Aaron; there is also the Messiah of Israel. I have already tied the Messiah of Aaron with the star out of Jacob who is also the Levite priest from Norwegian descent. This is the one who will be crowned by the stone (recall Joshua the high priest from Zechariah) in Jerusalem at the time that the third temple is built. This Messiah comes out of the house of Joseph through Nathan the son of David. The Messiah of Israel is the prince of the congregation who comes from the royal lineage of Solomon through Zerubbabel, a descendant of the cursed king, Conias (Jeconias). This Messiah is a man of strong British descent from the tribe of Judah. He is also of Dutch descent. He cannot sit on the throne of David in Jerusalem due to the curse. He will govern alongside the authority of the priestly Messiah, who will sit on the throne of David, in Jerusalem. They will rule as honorary rulers until their deaths which will precede the return of Jesus.

Another example from Professor Florentino García Martínez' research and writing follows...

CD

"22 blank And this is the rule of the assembly 23 [of the ca]mps. Those who walk in them, in the time of wickedness until there arises the messiah of Aaron1 and Israel, they shall be ten in number as a minimum to (form) thousands, hundreds, fifties 2and tens (CD XII 22-XIII 2; DSST 43). Blank and this is the exact interpretation of the regulations by which [they shall be ruled] 19 [until there arises the messiah] of Aaron and Israel 51. He shall atone for their sins [...pardon, and guilt] 9CD XIV 18-19; DSST 44). These shall escape in the age of the visitation; but those that remain shall be delivered up to the sword when there comes the messiah 11 of Aaron and Israel (CD XIX 10-11; DSST 45). And thus, all the men who entered the new 34 covenant in the land of Damascus and turned and betrayed and departed from the well of living waters, 35 shall not be counted in the assembly of the people and shall not be inscribed in their[lis]ts, from the day of the session7 of the unique Teacher until there arises the messiah of Aaron and Israel. Blank (CD XIX 33-XX7; DSST, 46).

As we have indicated, these four texts use one somewhat ambiguous expression: "Messiah of Aaron and Israel" in CD XII 23, 52 XIV 19 and XIX 10, and "Messiah of Aaron and of Israel" in CD XX1, an expression which can be translated both by "Messiah of Aaron and of Israel" and by "Messiah of Aaron and (Messiah)of Israel." Although the second expression can be interpreted more easily as referring to two different persons, 53 the possibility of interpreting both phrases as referring to a single person who comes from Aaron and Israel at the same time, is not only an actual possibility but it is also strengthened by the fact that in CD IX 19 the expression is followed by a verb in the singular. Accordingly, several scholars have made the "Messiah" the subject of the verb. And since the act is one of atonement, they have concluded that the figure indicated will be that of the "Priestly Messiah" who will atone for the sins of the people.54 But the text already cited, 1QS IX 11, resolves the ambiguity of the Hebrew expression. It proves that in all these cases the most likely interpretation is one which sees in these phrases a reference to the two "Messiahs" expected by the community." [19]

At this point I want to interject my own hypothesis on the identity crises between the probability of one or two Messiahs. There is a good possibility that there is one Messiah of Aaron and Israel. All this concludes is that one of these two may be of Levite lineage and still come from the royal line of Judah. One Messiah may be the Messiah of Aaron, the star out of Jacob, the crowned high priest of Norwegian descent through the lineage of Nathan yet still come from a royal line. Recall that the stone of Israel is to come out of Joseph in the end-time. This is the coronation stone that was in Britain for 700 years. It is possible that both of these Messiahs come from royal British descent. There may be a Messiah of Aaron and Israel as well as two separate Messiahs- The Messiah of Aaron and Israel and the Messiah of Israel.

Now I will begin a separate analysis of these two witnesses or Messiahs. First I will start with the priestly Messiah. Then after I have completed this, a more thorough understanding of the identities, characteristics, and responsibilities of these two "anointed" ones will have been established.

Example one of the priestly Messiah is found in Isaiah 49. "Listen, O Isles, unto me; and hearken, ye people, from far; The Lord hath called me from the womb; from the bowels of my mother hath he made mention of my name. And he hath made my mouth like a sharp sword; in the shadow of his hand hath he hid me, and made me a polished shaft; in his quiver hath he hid me; And said unto me, Thou art my servant, O Israel, in whom I will be glorified. Then I said, I have laboured in vain, I have spent my strength for nought, and in vain: yet surely my judgement is with the LORD, and my work with my God. And now, saith the LORD that formed me from the womb to be his servant, to bring Jacob again to him, Though Israel be not gathered, yet shall I be glorious in the eyes of the LORD and my God shall be my strength. And he said, it is a light thing that thou shouldest be my servant to raise up the tribes of Jacob, and to restore the preserved of Israel: I will also give thee for a light to the Gentiles, that thou mayest be my salvation unto the end of the earth." [20]

Another example of this Messiah can be found in Isaiah 53. "Who hath believed our report? and to whom is the arm of the LORD revealed? For he shall grow up before him as a tender plant, and as a root out of a dry ground: he hath no form or comeliness; and when we shall see him, there is no beauty that we should desire him. He is despised and rejected of men; a man of sorrows, and acquainted with grief: and we hid as it were our faces from him; he was despised and we esteemed him not Surely he hath borne our griefs, and carried our sorrows: yet we did esteem him stricken, smitten of God and afflicted. But he was wounded for our transgressions, he was bruised for our iniquities: the chastisement of our peace was upon him; and with his stripes we are healed. All we like sheep have gone astray; we have turned every one to his own way; and the LORD hath laid on him the iniquity of us all. He was oppressed, and he was afflicted, yet he opened not his mouth: he is brought as a lamb to the slaughter, and as a sheep before her shearers is dumb, so he openeth not his mouth. He was taken from prison and from judgement: and who shall declare his generation? for he was cut off out of the land of the living: for the transgression of my people was he stricken. And he made his grave with the wicked, and with the rich in his death; because he had done no violence, neither was any deceit in his mouth. Yet it pleased the LORD to bruise him: he hath put him to grief: when thou shalt make his soul an offering for sin, he shall see his seed, he shall prolong his days, and the pleasure of the LORD shall prosper in his hand. He shall see the travail of his soul, and shall be satisfied: by his knowledge shall my righteous servant justify many; for he shall bear their iniquities. Therefore will I divide him a portion with the great, and he shall divide the spoil with the strong;

because he hath poured out his soul unto death: and he was numbered with the transgressors; and he bare the sin of many, and made intercession for the transgressors." [21]

There has been much confusion pertaining to the identity of this suffering servant. Many have claimed that this is Jesus. Others have identified this servant with Israel. Although an element of truth is in both these assumptions there is evidence that ties this servant to the priestly Messiah and one of the two witnesses.

"a recently published text enables us to glimpse an independent development of the hope in the coming of the "priestly Messiah" as an agent of salvation at the end of times. It is an Aramic text, one of the copies of the Testament of Levi, recently published by E. Puech, which contains interesting parallels to chapter 19 of the Greek Testament of Levi included in the Testaments of the XII Patriarchs. From what can be deduced from the remains preserved, the protagonist of the work (probably the Patriarch Levi, although it cannot be completely excluded that it is Jacob speaking to Levi) speaks to his descendants in a series of exhortations. He also relates to them some of the visions, which have been revealed to him. In one of them, he tells them of the coming of a mysterious person. Although the text is hopelessly fragmentary it is of special interest since it seems to evoke the figure of a "priestly Messiah." This "Messiah" is described with the features of the suffering servant of Isaiah, as J. Starcky indicated in his first description of the manuscript. The longest and most important fragments of this new text can be translated as follows:

2.1 4Q541 fragment 9 col. 1

1[…] the sons of the generation […] 2[…] has wisdom. And he will atone for all the children of his generation, and he will be sent to all the children of 3 his people. His word is like the word of the heavens, and his teaching, according to the will of God. His eternal sun will shine 4 and his fire will burn in all the ends of the earth; above the darkness his sun will shine. Then darkness will vanish 5 from the earth, and gloom from the globe. They will utter many words against him, and an abundance of lies; they will fabricate fables against him. His generation will change the evil, 7 and [...] established in deceit and violence. The people will go astray in his days and they will be bewildered. "(DSST,270)" 22

I have already identified the Priestly Messiah with the coming Elijah. We have this Priestly Messiah who is also a suffering servant. There is more.

According to Bobby Rich, Author of The Last Prophet, "The final prophet makes it clear he has no strength, wealth, or earthly refuge and is totally dependent upon God for support, protection, and inspiration. He is chronically ill and has been at death's door at some point"23

Another example typifies the priestly Messiah. This will show how this Messiah witness may also be of the royal lineage of David and bypass the curse. Recall the curse of Jeconias that prevents a descendant from sitting on the throne of David, in Jerusalem.

Let's proceed to Micah. "But thou, Bethlehem Ephratah, though thou be little among the thousands of Judah, yet out of thee shall he come forth unto me that is to be ruler in Israel; whose goings forth have been from of old, from everlasting." 24 What can this mean? Who is the one out of Bethlehem Ephratah who shall rule? Does this refer to Jesus? Or does this refer to another Messiah?

According to Yair Davidy, world recognized authority in the field of lost Israelite identity, "Someone who belonged to the tribe of Ephraim was known as an Ephrathite i.e. in Hebrew, an "Ephrathi". This was the usual application of the term though a person living in Bethlehem of Judah could also be denoted as an "Ephrathi" since Bethlehem was in an area named "Ephrath". Eben Shushan in his authoritative Hebrew dictionary ("Ha Malon Ha chadash", Jerusalem, 1979, in Hebrew) lists alternative meanings for the name "Ephrathi".

"#Ephrathi 1 [derived from Ephrath meaning Bethlehem] a dweller of Ephrath: "Now David was the son of that Ephrathite of Bethlehem of Judah, whose name was Jesse..." (1 Samuel 17; 12).

"2. [derived from EPHRAIM] a member of the Tribe of Ephraim: "And Jeroboam the son of Nebat, an Ephrathite..." (1 Kings 11;26).

"3. [similised] aristocrat, honorable [so used due to the tribe of Ephraim who were considered the greatest and most respected of Tribes] "Every prince and great man that arose in Israel was given the name Ephrathi" (Pirkei de Rabbi Eliezer,45).

In Talmudic (e.g. Yalkut Shimeoni 1-Samuela;77) and Rabbinical Literature (Radak on 1Samuel 1;1) "Ephrathi" is taken to mean someone from the tribe of Ephraim or of noble birth or both." [25]

This adds evidence to support the expectation of a Messiah coming out of the house of Ephraim. Quite probably this person has lineage from the tribe of Ephraim, also, which can be traced back to British royalty. Remember Jeconias and the curse placed on his lineage. Recall Zedekiah, his Uncle. Strong evidence supports the theory that the prophet Jeremiah transported the stone of destiny and Zedekiah's daughters to Tara, Ireland. The lineage through Zedekiah was not cursed, but it was still of the royal line of Solomon. This priestly Messiah may have non-cursed, royal Davidic blood running through her veins as well as a Davidic lineage through Nathan. This would bypass the curse, and by right of inheritance this person would have every right to sit on the throne of David, in Jerusalem, and rule.

I have put together a portrait of the other Messiah witness. This Messiah is the expected Prince of the Congregation. He is of royal Davidic lineage, through Solomon, of the line of Zerubbabel. He can not sit on David's throne in Jerusalem because of the curse but; he will rule.

The first example of the Prince of the Covenant, the Sceptre out of Israel, can be found in Haggai. "Speak now to Zerubbabel the son of Shealtiel, governor of Judah, and to Joshua the son of Josedech, the high priest, and to the residue of the people, saying, who is left among you that saw this house in her first glory? and how do you see it now? is it not in your eyes in comparison of it as nothing? Yet now be strong, O

Zerubbabel, saith the LORD; and be strong, O Joshua, son of Josedech, the high priest; and be strong, all ye people of the land, saith the LORD and work: for I am with you, saith the LORD of hosts: According to the word that I covenanted with you when you came out of Egypt, so my spirit remaineth among you: fear ye not. For thus saith the LORD of hosts; Yet once, it is a little while, and I will shake the heavens, and the earth, and the sea, and the dry land; And I will shake all nations, and the desire of all nations shall come: and I will fill this house with glory, saith the LORD of hosts. The silver is mine, and the gold is mine, saith the LORD of hosts: and in this place will I give peace, saith the LORD of hosts." [26]

Zerubbabel is the coming prince that is of strong Judaic lineage. In this previous passage we see God calling Zerubbabel to begin construction of the temple. This is historic as well as futuristic. Zerubbabel built the second temple. A direct descendant of Zerubbabel will build the third temple in Jerusalem. This coming Messiah is the royal Davidic branch that comes to fulfill prophecy.

The Dead Sea Scrolls refer to this Prince. From Messianic Hopes in the Qumran Writings, Authored by Dr. Professor Florentino García Marínez, there is references to this person.

1.3 1Q28b (1Qsb) v20-29

"20 blank of the instructor. to bless the prince of the congregation, who [...] 21[...] And he will renew the covenant of the community for him, to establish the kingdom of his people for ever, [to judge the poor with justice] 22 to rebuke the humble of the earth with uprightness, to walk in perfection before him on all his paths [...] 23 to establish the [holy] covenant [during] the anguish of those seeking it. May the LORD raise you to an everlasting height, like a fortified tower upon the raised rampart. 24 May [you strike the peoples] with the power of your mouth. With your sceptre may you lay waste blank the earth. With the breath of your lips 25 may you kill the wicked. [May he send upon you a spirit of] counsel and of everlasting fortitude, a spirit blank of knowledge and of fear of God. May 26 your justice be the belt of [your loins, and loyalty] the belt of your hips. May he place upon you horns of iron and horseshoes of bronze. You will gore like a bull[...you will trample the peo]ples like mud of wheels. For God has established you as a sceptre. 28 Those who rule [...all the na]tions will serve you. He will make you strong by his Holy Name. 29 He will be like a li[on...] the prey from you with no one to hunt it. Your steads will scatter over (DSST, 433)."

"This lovely blessing of the "Prince of the Congregation" forms part of the collection of blessings included in the same manuscript that originally contained the Rule of the Community and the Rule of the Congregation. The blessing collects together the echoes from a whole series of texts which play an important role in the development of later messianic ideas, such as Numbers 24:17 and Genesis 49:9-10. But there is no doubt that Isaiah 11:1-5 provides the author with most of his ideas and expressions. The long introduction which proceeds the blessing proper (lines 20-23) where the figure of the "Prince of the Congregation" is described as the instrument chosen by God to "establish the kingdom of his people for ever" shows clearly that he is a traditional Messiah-King, although the technical term is not used. A conclusion which the very content of the blessing confirms in full: the twofold reference to the sceptre underlie its "royal" character and the references to Isaiah 11:1-5 stresses its davidic origin; his military functions are to the fore and stressed by the reference to Micah 4:13 in line 26 and all the nations end by submitting to him." [27]

Another example from the Bible is found in Haggai. "Speak to Zerubbabel, governor of Judah, saying, I will shake the heavens and the earth; And I will overthrow the throne of Kingdoms of the heathen; and I will overthrow the chariots, and those that ride in them; and the horses and their riders shall come down, every one by the sword of his brother. In that day, saith the LORD of hosts, will I take thee, O Zerubbabel, my servant, the son of Shealtiel, saith the LORD, and will make thee as a signet: for I have chosen thee, saith the LORD of hosts." [28]

More information on this Messiah witness is as follows..."And when he had gathered all the chief priests and scribes together, he demanded of them where Christ should be born. And they said unto him, In Bethlehem, in the land of Juda, art not the least among the princes of Juda: for out of thee shall come a governor, that shall rule my people Israel." [29]

Keep in mind that Christ means anointed. Though I identify this with someone other than Jesus, it is not blasphemy. This coming ruler is to be anointed by God as one of the last two Messiahs before the return of Jesus to rule the world. Jesus is the chief Messiah; he is not the only one.

One last example that points to this Princely ruler are the final words of Zebulon. Zebulon was one of the twelve sons of Jacob. Zebulon is identified with the country of Holland. The final words of Zebulon from the Testament of the Twelve Patriarchs are summarized as follows. I will be elevated again from out of my brothers; and I will rule in the midst of my people.[30] I will represent joy for those of my tribe that keep the Law of God. To the wicked the Lord will bring fire and destruction for ever. Here again, this princely ruler is identified with Zebulon. The Prince of the Congregation is a man in a high position who is of the tribe of Zebulon (Dutch), with strong Judaic lineage, and also comes from British royalty. This coming ruler will govern, with the priestly Messiah, the entire world for three and one half years.

Does Revelation speak of two witnesses or of two Messiahs? There is ample evidence presented in this chapter that consolidates the two concepts into one concrete and understandable concept. It is becoming clearly evident that two more "anointed" ones are to come with the power and spirit of God before the return of Jesus. Are these two people...Messiahs, empowered with the spirit and authority of God? Are they witnesses for Christ? Or are they both? Can these two concepts converge and make more sense? I will let you be the judge.

Chapter Sixteen

Messianic Prophecy-Making Sense of it All!

There is disagreement and argument between Jewish believers and Christian believers over who the Messiah is.[1] Most Jews do not believe Jesus was and is the Messiah because he did not fulfill all of the expectations that were required of the Jewish Messiah. Christians, typically, believe that Jesus was, and is, the Messiah, without question. Many believe that he is God himself, thanks to the gospel of Paul, although Jesus never claimed to be other than the Son of God. This disagreement is what separates Judaism from Christianity, along with basic doctrinal differences. The disagreement has valid arguments on both sides. What I intend to show, in this chapter, is how both religious institutions are correct and yet, they both miss the big picture. This is a conundrum to consider!

The Bible is full of messianic prophecy. These are far too numerous to mention all of them, so; I will list some of the most obvious ones to begin with to form an overview. Then, I will delve deeper into some controversial, little known messianic prophecies that Jesus predicted while fulfilling them at the same time. Jesus spoke in aphorisms and parables for the express purpose of concealing the truth of the kingdom from the majority of mankind. The Bible was meant to be understood at a designated level until the end of days when it was to be unsealed. This is the truth of the Bible. Remember hidden pictures that we all searched for as children in books? The book had hidden pictures within its pages, as does the Bible. This is the easiest way to explain it! Let's get to some prophecies of the Messiah...

The Messiah is to be of the lineage of Jacob and a star out of Jacob who would have dominion. Numbers 24:17-19

The Messiah is to be of the lineage of Judah. Genesis 49:10

The Messiah is to be a descendant of David and an heir to the throne. Isaiah 9:6-7, Jeremiah 33:15-18, II Samuel 12-13

The Messiah is to be the Son of God. Proverbs 30:4, Matthew 3:17

The Messiah is to come out of the house of Ephraim. Micah 5: 1-2 Did Jesus fulfill this one?

The spirit of God will anoint the Messiah. Isaiah 11:2, Matthew 3: 16

The Messiah will be a prophet like Moses. Deuteronomy 18: 15-18, Acts 3:20-22

The Messiah will come to announce liberty to the brokenhearted and prisoners, announcing the year of the Lord. Isaiah 35: 5-6, Isaiah 61: 1-2, Luke 4: 18-19

The Messiah will raise up the tribes of Jacob and restore the remnant of Israel. Isaiah 49: 6-8

The Messiah's ministry will include mending the breach of the gospel. Isaiah 42: 17-22

The Messiah will have a ministry in the Galilee of the Gentiles. Isaiah 9: 1-9, Matthew 4: 12-16

The Messiah is to be compassionate, tender, meek, and unostentatious. Isaiah 40:11, Isaiah 42: 3, Matthew 12: 15-20

The Messiah will carry the sin due others. Isaiah 53: 11-12

The Messiah will be a priest. Psalm 110:4

The Messiah will enter the temple with authority. Malachi 3:1, Haggai 2: 7-9, John 2:13-19

The Messiah will be hated and rejected without cause. Isaiah 49:7, Isaiah 53: 2-3, Mark 6: 3-4

The Messiah will be spat upon, beaten, and mocked. Isaiah 50:6, Psalm 22: 8-9, Matthew 26

The Messiah will be thirsty during his execution. Psalm 22:16, John 19: 18

The Messiah will be cut off for the sake of others. Daniel 9: 24- 26, Matthew 2:1

The Messiah will be the cornerstone of God's house. Psalm 118: 22-23, I Peter 2: 5-7

Many of these prophecies were fulfilled when Jesus came.[2] Christians believe that they were unequivocally fulfilled with Jesus- no questions asked. The problem with this assumption is that there are some prophecies that preclude Jesus from being the Messiah of the Jews in Jerusalem. There was a curse placed on the royal lineage of Judah through Jeconias- the line through which Jesus supposedly came.[3] This would prevent Jesus from sitting on the throne of David to rule from Jerusalem. How are we to reconcile these inconsistencies? Jesus fulfilled many messianic prophecies, but: he also spoke in parables. Why? Jesus was a Messiah, priest, and prophet. He predicted the future...

"And when he had gathered all the chief priests and scribes of the people together, he demanded of them where Christ should be born. And they said unto him, in Bethlehem, in the land of Judah: for out of thee shall come a Governor, that shall rule my people Israel."[4]

This refers to Jesus. He came from the house of Judah and governed Israel. Jesus became the Messiah of Israel, which includes the nations where Christian religion is concentrated. Although most of these Christians do not consider themselves Israelites, they are.

"Now when Jesus had heard that John was cast into prison, he departed into Galilee: And leaving Nazareth, he came and dwelt in Capernaum, which is upon the sea coast, in the borders of Zabulon and Nephthalim: That it might be fulfilled which was spoken by Esias the prophet, saying, the land of Zabulon, and the land of Nephthalim, by the way of the sea, beyond Jordon, Galilee of the Gentiles; The people which sat in darkness saw great light: and to them which sat in the region and shadow of death light is sprung up."[5]

Jesus ministry was to the Israelites yet here he speaks of the gentiles. What is obscure and oddly apparent is the words Zabulon and Nephthalim are Israelite tribes. Gentiles- in this context- means unconverted. Isaiah 9 was purposely fulfilled by Jesus to point out the origins of the last two anointed ones that were to come after him- the two witnesses.

"For unto us a child is born, unto us a son is given: and the government shall be upon his shoulder; and his name shall be called Wonderful, Counsellor, The mighty God, The everlasting Father, The Prince of Peace. Of the increase of his government and peace there shall be no end, upon the throne of David, and upon his kingdom, to order it, and to establish it with judgement and justice from henceforth even for ever. The zeal of the Lord of Hosts will perform this."[6]

Understand Jesus fulfilled this, at least partially. He was called God. He was called everlasting Father. He was given a kingdom. But lets explore this a little bit further.

According to Pastor Craig Lyons of Bet Emet Ministries, " there is an absence of to be verbs in Hebrew which makes this translation misleading. A second interpretation is the lack of the "to be" verbs (mentioned above) which when translated into English tend to make the uninitiated and uninformed reader believe the child is one and the same "being" by whose name he is called. These names are only intended to describe him and manifestations about him and his character. To say it another way, adjectives in a sentence describe the subject of the sentence. Just because the "child" (human child) is called Wonderful Counsellor, Mighty God, Everlasting Father, Prince of Peace" does not mean that he must be one and the same with the titles given him."[7]

This child is Jesus. This child is also the two coming anointed witnesses. Is this difficult to understand? There are three Messiahs. Jesus is the chief Messiah, always was, always will be! This is the truth of the matter! Jesus came; he died, and raised to life after 3 days. The two witnesses come; they die, and are raised to life after 3 days![8]

Jesus came to seek the lost sheep of Israel. His message was initially to the twelve tribes of Israel that were scattered at the time of Jesus. Recall the Assyrian and Babylonian captivity of the Israelites 400 years plus prior to the advent of Jesus. A good example of this can be found in Luke.

"And Joseph also went up from Galilee out of the city of Nazareth, into Judea, unto the city of David, which is called Bethlehem; (because he was of the house and lineage of David:)" [9]

Translated, this says that part of the house of Joseph would return to Jerusalem at some time because Joseph was of the lineage of David. This explains the parable of the prodigal son returning after much riotous living. It is predicting the last days just prior to the return of Jesus. It pertains specifically to Ephraim and Dan because they are omitted from being sealed in Revelation. [10] They either serve God completely or are destroyed. These two tribes have infiltrated much of our world today. They are extremely powerful. While there are people around the globe who carry genetics from these two tribes, they converged particularly in Britain, Wales, Scotland, Northern Ireland, the Netherlands, Denmark, Norway, and parts of Sweden.

These are just some of the prophecies from the Bible that can be interpreted or misinterpreted. The last Authorized Version of the Bible was the King James Version 1611. Other versions since this one have omitted key elements that completely destroy the context of the Bible. Let us assume that the British knew something when this book was written because they did. They were unwilling to come outright with the knowledge they possessed because it could have placed them in jeopardy. From the original Hebrew until the King James Version there have been other translations. After the King James Version there have been numerous translations which serve to distort the book because the translators did not know what they were reading. The Bible is an anthology of different languages, prophetic authors, and religions that are tied together by several common threads- Judah, Israel, the stone, the prophets, the gentiles, Jesus, and the Kingdom of God. These threads serve to form an abstract of a whole that many do not accept. Why do you suppose the Jews rejected Jesus as their Messiah?

The Jews did not, and cannot, for the most part, accept Jesus as their Messiah.[11] There are numerous reasons for their refusal to accept him, all of them valid. When the Jewish Messiah(s) come, several things will occur. First, Elijah must come forward. The temple in Jerusalem must be rebuilt. The lost tribes of Israel must be regathered to Zion. Then, the law will be taught from Jerusalem. The Levitical Holy days will be re-established and observed worldwide. None of this has occurred. Why?

Jesus was unable to fulfill all of the requirements of the Jewish Messiah due to human disobedience. Moses struck the anointed rock two too many times.[12] Moses was a great prophet with much authority and power. His disobedience created a situation where history was altered and prolonged. Jesus was unable to rule from Jerusalem. Jesus was unable to gather the lost sheep of Israel back to Jerusalem along with the stone, which was also lost at that time. Moses created a situation where two more Messiahs, empowered by God, must come to fulfill prophecy.

Two more Messiahs are coming! [13] They will come from the house of Joseph. They are connected by royal lineage to the stone of Israel- the coronation stone. They come from the tribe of Judah, as well as from other tribes. They are undoubtedly Christian. They will realize the error of their sins and repent before God and the world. These two anointed witnesses come to show the world that Jesus was and is the coming Messiah. They proclaim the Day of the Lord. They proclaim the true gospel and regather the world, all that will listen, back to a righteous Israelite faith. They bring Jacob's anointed Bethel stone home to become the cornerstone of the temple. God's word and authority will come from Jerusalem. Could anything be any clearer? [14]

"The Lord also shall save the tents of Judah first, that the glory of the house of David and the glory of the inhabitants of Jerusalem do not magnify themselves against Judah. In that day shall the Lord defend the inhabitants of Jerusalem; and he that is feeble among them at that day shall be as David; and the house of David shall be as God, as the angel of the Lord before them. And it shall come to pass in that day, that I will seek to destroy all the nations that come against Jerusalem, the spirit of grace and of supplications: And they shall look upon me whom they have pierced, and they shall mourn for him, as one mourneth for his only son, and shall be in bitterness for him, as one that is in bitterness for his firstborn." [15]

Interpreting the Bible has baffled intellectuals since it was written. The reason for this is human blindness. The Bible is a literary anthology. It is a work of literary genius orchestrated by the God of the universe. The book must be interpreted as a coherent whole from start to finish. This is how it is inspired and infallible. The Bible is a history book. As a history book, it must have a beginning, middle, and an end. The Bible is a prophecy book. Because the prophets of God were anointed, their actions and words were of tremendous consequence. Everything the prophets said and did predicted the future. And because of prophets, the prophecies must all be fulfilled and have an end. This is God's Bible; and the word of God comes through prophets! It is a Bible full of history, prophecy, and fulfillment.

Our Father which art in heaven, Hallowed be thy name. Thy Kingdom come. Thy will be done in earth, as it is in heaven. Give us this day our daily bread. And forgive us our debts, as we forgive our debtors. And lead us not into temptation, but deliver us from evil: For thine is the kingdom, and the power, and the glory, Forever. Amen!" [16]

Chapter Seventeen

The Gospel of the Kingdom

"And this gospel of the kingdom shall be preached in all the world for a witness unto all nations; and then shall the end come."1

"For nation shall rise against nation, and kingdom against kingdom: And there shall be earthquakes in divers places, and there shall be famines and troubles: these are the beginnings of sorrows. But take heed to yourselves: for they shall deliver you up to councils; and in the synagogues ye shall be beaten: and ye shall be brought before rulers and kings for my sake, for a testimony against them. And the gospel must first be published among all nations."2

This gospel of the kingdom has not been published or preached as a witness.3 If it had been, the end would have come and Jesus would have returned with all of his faithful followers. Somewhere, somehow, the Bible has been misinterpreted and manipulated to placate the masses. The laws of God were not done away with; such implication only complicates the true gospel of the kingdom making it virtually impossible to correctly decipher and understand. Jesus was a Jew who observed the Jewish holy days and the Sabbath. He didn't come to do away with the laws but to fulfill them. He did this by becoming the perfect example for all humanity to follow. He was the chosen Messiah because of his perfection and complete humility and submission to God's authority. What exactly happened to the gospel as Jesus taught it?

Soon after Jesus died, differences in religious dogma infiltrated the churches and divisions became prevalent within different sects. Then, Paul, who met Jesus only in a vision, came preaching his own gospel-the gospel of grace. While this gospel had validity or it wouldn't have been in the Bible, Israel became, first, a side issue, then, it went into obscurity. Paul's gospel came to be known as the dispensation of grace. For 2000 years, this gospel has been preached. It goes as follows: Jesus came as the perfect sacrifice for our sins, was raised to life three days later, and now sits next to God in heaven as the Messiah intercessor for all of us. This message has just about finished targeting its intended audience. The purpose of the gospel of grace was to humble sinners into repentance, not to give license for all unrepentant sinners to continue tosin. The gospel of the kingdom was put on hold after Jesus died. What gospel did Jesus come to preach?

"Therefore say, Thus saith the Lord God; I will even gather you from the people, And assemble you out of the countries where you have been scattered, and I will give you the land of Israel. And they shall come thither, and they shall take away all the detestable things thereof from thence. And I will give them one heart, And I will put a new spirit within you; and I will take the stony heart out of their flesh: That they may walk in my statutes, and keep mine ordinances, and do them: and they shall be my people, and I will be their God. But as for them whose heart walketh after the heart of their detestable things and their abominations, I will recompense their way upon their own heads, saith the Lord God."[4]

This is the gospel of the kingdom that Jesus came to teach. He came to seek the lost sheep of Israel, who had been scattered after the kingdom of David fell into ruins and went into captivity. Approximately 400 years had elapsed from the time the captivity was complete until the arrival of Jesus. Jesus came to find the scattered Israelites and the stone of Israel to return them to Jerusalem and reunite them with Judah. Jesus came to rule over them as the lawful Messiah from the line of David; a legitimate son of God.

After the two witnesses arrive to demonstrate the authority and power of God, Jesus will return. Jesus died before his mission was complete. The two witnesses do not come to preach Jesus in the manner that traditional Christian ministers do. If that was their purpose, there would be no need for their arrival. They arrive on the scene in Jerusalem when uncertainty and confusion is prevalent worldwide. They straighten out the error of understanding that has led the nations astray. They clarify the end from the beginning. They reunite the divided houses of Israel- "the lost sheep."

"And I will strengthen the house of Judah, and I will save the house of Joseph, and I will bring them again to place them; for I have mercy upon them: and they shall be as though I had not cast them off: for I am the Lord their God, and will hear them. And they of Ephraim shall be like a mighty man, and their heart shall rejoice as though wine: yea, their children shall see it, and be glad; their heart shall rejoice in the Lord, I will hiss for them, and gather them; for I have redeemed them: and they shall increase as they have increased. And I will sow them among the people: and they shall remember me in far countries, and they shall live with their children, and turn again."[5]

"The remnant shall return, even the remnant of Jacob, unto the mighty God. For though thy people Israel be as the sand of the sea, yet a remnant of them shall return: the consumption decreed shall over flow with righteousness."[6]

"Behold, I will bring them from the North country, and gather them from the coasts of the earth, and with them the blind and the lame, the woman with child, and her that travaileth with child together: a great company shall return thither. They shall come with weeping, and with supplications will I lead them: I will cause them to walk by the rivers of waters in a straight way, wherein they shall not stumble: for I am a father to Israel, and Ephraim is my firstborn. Hear the word of the

LORD, O ye nations and declare it in the isles afar off, And say, He that scattereth Israel will gather him, and keep him, as a shepherd doth his flock. For the LORD hath redeemed Jacob, and ransomed him from the hand of him that was stronger than he."[7]

The two witnesses arrive at the conclusion of the dispensation of grace. They bring the stone of Israel home, oversee the building of the temple in Jerusalem, bring the faithful of Jacob home, reinstate the holy days, and serve as honorary priest and Messiahs. They warn all nations to follow the example of Jesus and keep the law of God, so that they may be saved. They warn people of all nations not to take the mark of the beast that will be required immediately after they are killed. They are killed by the antichrist that immediately proceeds to sit in the reconstructed temple claiming to be God, demanding that all worship him and take his mark, or die. After the two witnesses die, they are resurrected 3 ½ days later followed by the seventh trumpet at which the faithful saints of God and Christ are also resurrected. This is the true gospel of the kingdom! [8]

About the Author

Susan Alfson holds a Ph.D. in Philosophy in the field of Biblical Studies. This is her first book written in this field. She is currently working on her second book.

Notes

CHAPTER ONE NOTES:

[1] Revelation 11:3-6, AV: This is the only place in the Bible where two witnesses are mentioned.

[2] Why are two more prophets needed? In the Bible, prophets are always divinely inspired messengers who foresee the future and lead the righteous back to God.

[3] See R.H. Charles, *"Apocalypse of Baruch,"* *64,* Principate of my Messiah?

[4] Deuteronomy 18:15; 17-19, AV: The next Elijah?

[5] Revelation 11:11-12, AV: They are raised to life after three and one half days.

[6] Revelation 11:1, AV, They initiate the building of the next temple.

[7] See Seymour Rossel, *"Introduction to Jewish History,"* 56.

[8] The words of prophets must always be heeded.

[9] Zechariah 4:11-14, AV, Two anointed ones.

[10] Matthew 20:21,AV.

[11] Matthew 20:23,AV.

[12] See Yair Davidy, *"The Tribes," This* book contains excellent reference material to the modern day descendants of Israel.

[13] See Matthew 22:14,AV

[14] Isaiah 46: 6-7, AV.

[15] Haggai 2: 21-23, AV.

CHAPTER TWO NOTES:

[1] Genesis 28:10-15,AV: Jacob's descendants became very numerous and spread across the earth; A remnant will return to Jerusalem.

[2] Genesis 28:13, AV.

[3] Genesis 28: 18-22, AV: In this context could pillar mean witness?

[4] Bethel is an area in the West bank of Israel that the Palestinians desire.

[5] The regathering of Israel is not yet complete.

[6] Genesis 49: 5-7, AV: This refers to Ephraim.

[7] Where is the majority of the descendants of Jacob today?

[8] Israel was forced to move many times.

[9] Genesis 48: 19, AV: Ephraim inherits the birthright, which includes the land and the scepter.

[10] Genesis 49: 3-4, AV.

[11] Genesis 49: 5-7, AV.

[12] Genesis 49: 8-10, AV.

[13] Genesis 49: 13, AV.

[14] Genesis 49:15,AV.

[15] Genesis 49: 16-18, AV.

[16] Genesis 49: 19, AV.

[17] Genesis 49: 18, AV

[18] Genesis 49: 21, AV.

[19] Genesis 49: 22-24,AV: The stone of Israel?

[20] Genesis 49: 27, AV.

CHAPTER THREE NOTES:

[1] See Lambert Dolphin, "The Mainline Covenants Of Yahweh," available from http://www.1dolphin.org/Maincov.html Internet; accessed 13 August 1998.

[2] Different covenants were established during different periods of history; each dispensation had its own prophet chosen by God.

[3] See A.N. Wilson, "*Paul: The Mind of the Apostle,*" to get an idea how Paul so ingeniously promoted Christianity.

[4] See, " ANE History: The Davidic Covenant," available from http://www.theology.edu/lec16.htm Internet; accessed 4 March 1999.

[5] See Matthew 18: 11-14, AV.

[6] Matthew 9: 35,AV.

[7] Mark 1: 14-15,AV.

[8] See Craig Lyons, "Can We Truthfully Say Yeshua Is The Messiah... Yet?" available from http://.../CAN%20WE%20TRUTHFULLY%20SAY%20JESUS%20IS%2oMESSIAH.ht Internet; accessed 25 April 2000.

[9] See, "The Eight Biblical Covenants," available from http://www.pond.net/~tio/bible/cove_bib.htm Internet; accessed 12 November 1998.

[10] See Lambert Dolphin, "The Mainline Covenants Of God".

[11] Genesis 12: 2-3, AV.

[12] Exodus 19: 3-5, AV.

[13] Jeremiah 31: 31-33, AV.

[14] This will all come to a conclusion during the Apocalypse.

[15] II Samuel 7:8-13, AV.

[16] See E. Raymond Capt, "*Jacob's Pillar*," 81.

[17] II Samuel 7: 13-16, AV.

CHAPTER FOUR NOTES:

[1] II Samuel 3:2-5,AV.

[2] II Samuel 5:14-16, AV.

[3] Nathan is also a son of David associated with Benjamin, the sons of Zadok, and prophecy; In the New Testament we find that Nathan is also of the line of the anointed.

[4] II Samuel 7: 2-6, AV.

[5] II Samuel 7: 11,AV.

[6] I Kings 1:1-11,AV.

[7] I Kings 1: 32-35,AV.

[8] I Kings 2:4,AV.

[9] The throne of David is the stone of Israel.

[10] I Kings 1: 35,AV.

[11] I Chronicles 22:9-10,AV.

[12] See Lambert Dolphin, " *The Temple of Solomon.*"

[13] I Kings 9: 3-5,AV.

[14] I Kings 9:6-7,AV.

[15] See Bobby Rich, "*The Last Prophet,*" 37.

[16] Israel is about to move its throne once again; it will be taken to Jerusalem where the third temple is to be built.

[17] Many people believe Israel is comprised of only the Jews- not so; there are twelve tribes of Israel.

[18] "King Solomon's Era – Israel's Golden Age," available from: http://www.intournet.co.il/holyland/vol4-1-1.html ; Internet; accessed 9 September 20.

CHAPTER FIVE NOTES:

[1] See "Abraham's Legacy – Extent of Solomon's Kingdom," available from http://www.bibleprophecy.org/abrahams/solomon.html Internet; accessed 4 April 1999; Also see, "Solomon's Kingdom," available from http://www.execulink.com/~wblank/solkingd.htm Internet; accessed 29 September 2000.

[2] See J. LLewellyn Thomas FRCS, "*The Invasions and Deportations of Israel,*" 5-47.

[3] II Kings 19: 25-32, AV.

[4] See E. Raymond Capt, "*Missing Links Discovered in Assyrian Tablets,*" 7.

[5] See "The Hebrews—Exile," available from
http://www.wsu.edu/~dee/HEBREWS/EXILE/HTM Internet;
accessed 7 August 2000.

[6] Seymour Rossel, *"Introduction to Jewish History".*

[7] II Kings 23,AV.

[8] Jeremiah 22:29-30, AV.

[9] This promise comes through the lineage of Nathan.

[10] II Samuel 7:11-14, AV.

[11] II Samuel 7: 16, AV.

[12] This promise means that the throne, kingdom, and house of David had to have been re-established somewhere other than Jerusalem.

[13] I Kings 9: 6-7, AV.

[14] I Chronicles 22: 9-10, AV.

[15] Douglas C Nesbit, BA., "Bethel – Part IV, Anointed Stone," available from http://www.british-israel-world-fed.ca/Brit155.html Internet; accessed 25 April 2000.

CHAPTER SIX NOTES:

[1] See, "Bible History Timeline," available from
http://www.konig.org/CIFtimeline.htm Internet; accessed 27 March 2000.

[2] The Bible has always seen struggles between the Israelites and the Romans.

[3] The British helped the Jews to re-establish a homeland in Jerusalem.

[4] See J. LLewellyn Thomas, FRCS, *"The Assyrian Invasions and Deportations of Israel".*

[5] II Kings 15: 19-20, AV.

[6] II Kings 15:29, AV.

[7] See E. Raymond Capt, *"Missing Links Discovered In Assyrian Tablets,"* 67.

8 Ibid.

9 II Kings 17: 18-20, AV.

10 Deuteronomy 11: 12, AV.

11 E Raymond Capt explains this in, "*Missing Links Discovered In Assyrian Tablets*".

12 II Kings 18:13, AV.

13 Yair Davidy writes about this in, "*Ephraim,*" He has done extensive research in the field of lost Israelite identity.

14 See, "The Last Days: Section 6: The Kingdom," available from http://www.bbie.org/english/resources/last_days/chap26.html Internet; accessed 30 September 2000.

CHAPTER SEVEN NOTES:

1 See E. Raymond Capt, "*Missing Links Discovered In Assyrian Tablets,*" 75,97,99.

2 See E. Raymond Capt, "*Missing Links Discovered In Assyrian Tablets,*" 120, 121.

3 Ibid.

4 II Esdras 13: 40-45, APOCRYPHA.

5 Tobit 1:1-3, APOCRYPHA.

6 See R.H. Charles, "*The Apocalypse of Baruch,*" 124-166; this is an epistle written to the lost tribes of Israel.

7 See Yair Davidy, "*The Tribes,*" 249; Yair Davidy is a Jewish scholar who has extensively researched the migrations of the lost tribes of Israel.

8 Jeremiah 31: 20-21, AV.

9 See Yair Davidy, "*Ephraim,*"130-131.

10 See Yair Davidy, "*The Tribes,*" 50; 64.

11 Ibid.

12 See E Raymond Capt, "*Missing Links Discovered In Assyrian Tablets,*" 157.

13 Ibid, 203.

14 See, "Israel's Symbol and Heraldry," available from http://asis.com/~stag/symbols.html Internet; accessed 12 April 2000.

15 See Yair Davidy, *"The Tribes".*

16 Ephraim is associated with Britain.

CHAPTER EIGHT NOTES:

1 See Dr. Ray Stedman, "The 400 Years Between the Old and New Testaments," available from: http://www.best.com/~dolphin/0240.html Internet; accessed 29 march 1999.

2 See Andrew Gray, *"The Origin and Early History of Christianity in Britain".*

3 See "Biblical Jerusalem," available from http://gurukul.ucc.american.edu/TED/hpages/jerusalem/biblical.htm Internet; accessed 24 April 1999.

4 See John J. Collins, *"The Scepter and the Star- The Messiahs of the Dead Sea Scrolls and other Ancient Literature,"* 20-48.

5 See "How Can Jesus Sit on David's Throne when it's Cursed?" available from http://www.pe.net/~lennyesp/bibi_cntr/con080.htm Internet; accessed 18 April 1999.

Also see, "Was Jesus the Messiah?" available from http://www.geocities.com/athens/5338/debate4.html Internet; accessed 8 December 1998.

6 Matthew 10: 5-6, AV.

7 Ibid.

8 Ibid.

9 See CF Balslev, "Bible History," 86.

10 Matthew 1:11-16, AV, another lineage through Nathan is given in Luke which makes Jesus' lineage ambiguous and speculative; some argue that Jesus was born of God so no Davidic lineage was

required; Jesus' place of birth was also shrouded in mystery-Nazareth or Bethlehem- does it matter? Also see David Donnini, "Gamla," available from http://www.donnini.com/naza-eng.htm Internet; accessed 24 April 2000, Did Jesus(or somebody else) intentionally conceal his lineage and place of birth?

[11] See Revelation 5:5, AV, If Jesus was only an adopted son of the Davidic lineage, who is this lion from the tribe of Judah that breaks the seals of prophecy?; Are we to know anything for certain other than to obey God by keeping his commandments and accept his pardon through the sacrifice of his son, Jesus?

[12] I Corinthians 10:1-4, AV.

[13] See E Raymond Capt, "*Jacob's Pillar*," 8.

[14] Exodus 17: 5-6, AV.

[15] Numbers 20:11, AV.

[16] Moses disobeyed which resulted in extended history and the present "church" age.

[17] Two witnesses come to Jerusalem to fulfill the prophetic action of Moses striking the rock two more times; they come to finish the incomplete work of Jesus.

[18] Matthew 16: 15-19, AV.

[19] Genesis 49: 21, AV.

[20] Isaiah 9: 1-2, 6, AV.

[21] Matthew 5: 17-18, AV.

[22] Matthew 12: 17-19, AV.

[23] Matthew 4: 13-16, AV.

[24] Zebulun is associated with Holland while Naphtali is associated with Norway; the two anointed witnesses are descended from these countries.

[25] Matthew 22: 42-44, AV.

[26] The stone was recently moved from England to Scotland in 1996.

[27] See AN. Wilson, "*Paul: The Mind of the Apostle*," 72.

28 Jesus never preached the gospel that Paul promoted-Jesus sought only the lost sheep of Israel.

29 Jesus died before Paul became a disciple.

30 II Peter 3: 13-17, AV.

31 A stone of mysterious repute arrives in Tara Ireland around 584 BC.

CHAPTER NINE NOTES:

1 Genesis 49: 8-10, AV.

2 See E. Raymond Capt, *"Jacob's Pillar,"* 25.

3 Genesis 38: 27-30, AV.

4 Pharez has always been the royal line of Judah.

5 The stone of Israel was planted in Tara, Ireland in 584 BC. with Zedekiah's daughters; according to history, Zarah was already there.

6 This is assuming she married into her own house and had sons to continue the line.

7 Jeremiah 43: 5-7, AV.

8 The royal line of Judah was always sought out for extermination.

9 See JC. Gawler, *"Dan, The Pioneer of Israel"*.

10 This served to strengthen Judah.

11 Nathan was a brother and servant to Solomon; Nathan is mentioned in the New Testament as one of the lines through which Christ descends.

12 See, "The Trojan Origins of European Royalty," available from http://triumph.simplenet.com/1000109a.htm Internet; accessed 12 February 1998.

13 Genesis 49: 8, AV.

14 Deuteronomy 33: 22, AV.

15 See Yair Davidy, *"The Tribes,"* 63.

16 The house of David.

CHAPTER TEN NOTES:

[1] Jeremiah 31: 8-9, AV.

[2] Ephraim was given the birthright by Jacob.

[3] Ezekiel 37: 16-17, AV.

[4] Ezekiel 37: 21-22, AV.

[5] Jeremiah 31: 20-21, AV.

[6] Some of these monuments may go back as far as Moses, perhaps further.

[7] See Yair Davidy, "*Ephraim,*" 134-135.

[8] Zechariah 10: 6-8, AV.

[9] Jacob blessed Joseph's sons, Ephraim and Manasseh, but the birthright went to Ephraim.

[10] Britain, France, the Netherlands, Sweden, Denmark, and Norway have all had kingdoms; only Britain had the anointed coronation stone.

[11] See, "United Israel- Were the Lost Tribes Ever Really Lost," available from http://www.unitedisrael.org/ten-tribes-israel-ever-lost.html Internet; accessed 3 October 2000.

[12] Jacob's Pillar is a very important theme of the Bible.

[13] Scotland claimed ownership of this rock for many years; England gave it back in 1996.

[14] This is thought by many to be the United States of America.

[15] The strength of Israel has always been the law of God.

[16] Matthew 22: 42- 44, AV; this specifies that God's earthly kingdom has always existed but the authority appears to go with the rock!

CHAPTER ELEVEN NOTES:

[1] See Zechariah 12:10; Also see, "The Key of David," available from http://www.do-you-love-me.org/wsomers/thekey.html Internet; accessed 12 August 1999.

[2] See, "Nathan," available from http://bibletutor.luthersem.edu/bibletutorlive/people/nathan.htm Internet; accessed 5 April 1999.

[3] I Chronicles 17: 3-5, AV.

[4] I Chronicles 17: 11-14, AV.

[5] II Samuel 7: 12-16, AV.

[6] Jesus said in the New Testament, "Upon this rock I will build my church," and so he did.

[7] The Bible is full of double meaning intended for different historical periods.

[8] Revelation 3: 7-10, AV.

[9] England is in a strategic position where invasion after invasion has occurred, The Vikings came from the north; the Jutes came; the Anglo-Saxons came; the Normans came; they all merged into one people; See Morgan Llywelyn, *"The Vikings in Ireland".*

[10] Jeremiah 30:7, AV.

[11] II Chronicles 7: 17-20, AV.

[12] The servant would become the ruler- Nathan served Solomon loyally throughout the Bible; One country that has stood behind England with dogged dedication is Norway.

[13] This could apply to many European countries.

[14] Genesis 35: 11, AV.

[15] The Scandinavian countries are known for this.

[16] I Kings 2: 44-46, AV.

[17] See Yair Davidy, *"The Tribes,"* 209.

[18] See Yair Davidy, *"Ephraim,"* for a thorough discussion of the Scandinavian's identities.

[19] See Yair Davidy, *"The Tribes,"* 97.

[20] See Yair Davidy, *"The Tribes,"* 211.

[21] See Yair Davidy, *"Ephraim,"* 141.

[22] Genesis 35: 11-15, AV.

CHAPTER TWELVE NOTES:

[1] See Matthew 16: 16-19, AV.

[2] Exodus 17: 4-6, AV.

[3] Numbers 20: 7-11, AV.

[4] Isaiah 48: 20-21, AV.

[5] Endtime prophecy concerning this rock is found in Genesis 49 where Jacob predicted that the stone of Israel would come out of Joseph (England)? Also see, "The Stone of Destiny", available from http://www.aboutscotland.com/stone/destiny.html Internet; accessed 5 October 2000.

[6] Jacob anointed this rock; it would make little sense to leave it behind on his travels; Also see, "Did You Know? –Stone of Destiny- The Coronation Stone", available from http://www.scottishcul-ture.about.com/aboutuk/scottishculture/library/blknow Internet; accessed 5 October 2000.

[7] See "Bible History Timeline," available from http://www.konig.org/ciftiimeline.htm Internet; accessed 4 January 1999.

[8] See I Corinthians 10: 1-4, AV.

[9] Joshua 24: 27, AV.

[10] II Kings 12: 12- 14, AV, Judah was separate from Israel and had the rock until right before the Babylonian captivity.

[11] See E. Raymond Capt, "*Jacob's Pillar*," 29; a mysterious rock appears in Tara, Ireland in 584 BC., Also see, "Stone of Destiny", available from http://www.iwc.net/~levi/stone.htm Internet; accessed 7 September 2000.

[12] Jeremiah 1:10, AV.

[13] II Maccabees 2: 4-7, APOCRYPHA.

[14] See E Raymond Capt, "*Jacob's Pillar*," 55.

[15] See E Raymond Capt, "*Jacob's Pillar*," 29.

[16] Ibid.

[17] Ibid.

[18] Ibid.

[19] See E Raymond Capt, *"Jacob's Pillar,"* 55.

[20] Matthew 21: 42- 43, AV; Also see, "The Stone of Destiny," available from http://www.pictphd.demon.co.uk/spm/news_09.htm Internet; accessed 5 October 2000.

[21] I Corinthians 10: 1-4, AV.

[22] England is the site of Glastonbury Abbey, the legendary first Christian church outside of Jerusalem.

[23] Mathew 17: 15-18, AV.

[24] Ephesians 2: 19-21, AV.

[25] Isaiah 29: 16, AV.

[26] See Andrew Gray, *"The Origin and Early History of Christianity In Britain".*

[27] See, "Glastonbury Abbey and the Legends of Joseph of Arimathea and King Arthur," available from http://www.britannia.com/history/abbey.html Internet; accessed 16 June 2000.

[28] Matthew 21: 44, AV.

[29] Isaiah 28: 16, AV.

[30] Daniel 2: 44-45, AV.

CHAPTER THIRTEEN NOTES:

[1] Daniel 2: 40-45, AV.

[2] Jerusalem will soon become the center of world authority; see Revelation 11.

[3] Daniel 2: 31-35, AV.

[4] The fourth kingdom of Daniel is forming; keep your eye on the European Monetary Union where this kingdom is originating; See, "The Truth About Europe," available from http://members.tripod.com/~eurotruth/11.htm Internet; accessed 22 February 2000.

[5] This seems to point to Ephraim, Dan, Judah, and Levi, sons of Zadok (a priestly line), and descendants of Nathan, Also see, "Vote

Could Signal Start of Two Tier Europe," available from http://www.cnn.com/2000/WORLD/europe/09/28/oakley.analysis/ Internet; accessed 28 September 2000.

6 Christ means more than Jesus; Christ is the forming "anointed" stone kingdom that usurps authority out of the hands of the leaders of the fourth kingdom; the antichrist will be a man- as well as his followers- who oppose God's anointed authority.

7 Daniel 2: 40-45, AV, See "Endtime Bible Prophecy," available from http://www.flash.net/~venzor/danielkingdom.htm Internet; accessed 17 September 1999.

8 This has far reaching implications; Will the antichrist and false prophet be leading actors in U.S. politics? See "Ties and Tensions: EU Relations with the United States," available from http://www.eurunion.org/infores/euguide/chapter5.htm Internet; accessed 19 February 2000.

9 See "Four EU Countries Outside EMU," available from http://www.rferl.org/nca/features/1998/12/F.RU.981214142936.ht ml accessed 2 October 2000, Also see, "Norway Outside the EU," available from http://www.bullen.demon.co.uk/cibnor.htm Internet; accessed 6 September 1999.

10 See Bill Jamieson, "Britain's Global Future," available from http://www.independenceuk.org.uk/cgi/ukip.pl?id=33 Internet; accessed 4 December 1999.

11 See Andrew Marr, "The Spectator, 5 February 2000" available from http://www.bfors.com/press/news/20000402z.html ,Internet; accessed 22 February 2000.

12 Britain is in a precarious situation as all sovereignty is slowly being stripped away.

13 See Andrew Marr, "The Spectator," 5 February 2000.

14 Ezekiel 37: 16-22, AV.

15 See Bobby Rich, *"The Last Prophet,"* 53.

16 Jeremiah 31: 8-10, AV.

CHAPTER FOURTEEN NOTES:

[1] Malachi 4: 5-6, AV.

[2] See, "The Appearance of Elijah," available from http://www.voicenet.com/~lelgee/writings/elijah-1.html Internet; accessed 6 October 2000.

[3] I Kings 17: 1, AV.

[4] I Kings 18: 37-39, AV.

[5] Matthew 11: 7-10, AV.

[6] Ezekiel 2; 3;7, AV.

[7] Daniel 12: 4, AV.

[8] Revelation 10: 2-4, AV.

[9] See Bobby Rich, *"The Last Prophet,"*50-51.

[10] See Yair Davidy, *"Ephraim,"* 253-254.

[11] See Bobby Rich, *"The Last Prophet,"*10-11.

[12] See Bobby Rich, *"The Last Prophet,"* 53-54.

[13] Habakkuk 2: 1-3, AV.

[14] See Bobby Rich, *"The Last Prophet,"* 56-58.

[15] See Florentino García Martínez, *"The Dead Sea Scrolls Translated-IQHXV 1-6".*

[16] See Florentino Garcia Martinez, "Messianic Hopes In The Qumran Writings,"- chapter 5-pg 2, available from http://www.kbyu.org/deadsea/book/chapter5/intro.html Internet; accessed 15 February 1999.

[17] Numbers 25: 17-19, AV.

CHAPTER FIFTEEN NOTES:

[1] See Revelation 11.

[2] See Zechariah 5: 12-14, AV.

[3] Numbers 24: 14-19, AV.

[4] Isaiah 9: 1-7, AV.

[5] Two anointed rulers descend from the countries of Norway and the Netherlands.

[6] See Yair Davidy, *"The Tribes,"* 200.

[7] See Yair Davidy, *"The Tribes,"* 320.

[8] Jeremiah 33: 14-18, AV.

[9] The elect of Israel.

[10] Zechariah 3: 1-9, AV.

[11] Zechariah 4, AV.

[12] Two anointed ones.

[13] Jeremiah 22: 28-30, AV.

[14] Zerubbabel was of the cursed line (Jeconias) of Solomon, God cannot allow him to sit on the throne in Jerusalem-but, he will have tremendous power.

[15] Luke 3: 31, AV.

[16] Mark 10: 37-40, AV.

[17] See Zechariah 4.

[18] See Florentino García Martínez, "Messianic Hopes in the Qumran Writings," 1-2, available from http://www.kbyu.org/deadsea/book/chapter5/sec5.html Internet; accessed 16 February 1999.

[19] See Florentino García Martínez, "Messianic Hopes in the Qumran Writings," 3-4, available from http://www.kbyu.org/deadsea/book/chapter5/sec5.html Internet; accessed 16 February 1999.

[20] Isaiah 49: 1-6, AV.

[21] Isaiah 53, AV, the suffering servant.

[22] See Florentino García Martínez, "Messianic Hopes in the Qumran Writings," 1-2, available from http://www.kbyu.org/deadsea/book/chapter5/sec3.html Internet; accessed 15 February 1999.

[23] See Bobby Rich, *"The Last Prophet,"* 55.

[24] Micah 5:2, AV.

[25] See Yair Davidy, *"Ephraim,"* 69-71.

[26] Haggai 2: 2-9, AV.

27 See Florentino García Martínez, "Messianic Hopes in the Qumran Writings," 1-2, available from http://www.kbyu.org/deadsea/book/chapter5/sec2.html Internet; accessed 15 February 1999.

28 Haggai 2: 21-23, AV.

29 Matthew 3: 4-6, AV.

30 See Helene Koppejan, "*Strange Parallel-Zebulun-Tribe of Israel*".

CHAPTER SIXTEEN NOTES:

1 See John J. Collins, "*The Scepter and the Star*," also see, Craig Lyons, "Can We Truthfully Say Yeshua Is The Messiah ...Yet?" available from http://.../CAN%20WE%20TRUTHFULLY%SAY%20SAY%20JESUS%20IS%20MESSIAH.ht Internet; accessed 25 April 2000.

2 See Noishe Rosen, "Yshua".

3 See Jeremiah 22:30, AV, also see, "Was Jesus the Messiah?" available from http://www.geocities.com/Athens/5338/debate4.html Internet; accessed 21 February 1999.

4 Matthew 3:4-6, AV.

5 Matthew 4:12-16, AV.

6 Isaiah 9:6-7, AV.

7 See Craig Lyons, "Isaiah 9:6 as Yeshua Would Have Understood It," available from http://faithofye.../a8%20ISA%209%206%20AS%20YESHUA%20UNDERSTOOD%20IT.ht Internet; accessed 15 October 1999.

8 See Revelation 11.

9 Luke 2:4, AV.

10 Revelation 7.

11 Many of the Jews were expecting two messiahs.

12 Numbers 20:11-12, AV.

13 See John J. Collins, "*The Scepter and the Star*," 74.

[14] See E. Raymond Capt, *"Jacob's Pillar"*.

[15] Zechariah 12: 7-10, AV.

[16] Matthew 6:9-13, AV.

CHAPTER SEVENTEEN NOTES:

[1] Matthew 24:14, AV.

[2] Mark 13:8-10, AV.

[3] The gospel of Paul has been preached and taught worldwide- this is better known as the dispensation of grace; it is not the gospel of the kingdom.

[4] Ezekiel 11:17-21, AV.

[5] Zechariah 10:6-9, AV.

[6] Isaiah 10:21-22, AV.

[7] Jeremiah 31:8-11, AV.

[8] This begins the 1000 year reign of Jesus with his faithful followers who will rule alongside Jesus in this kingdom.

Bibliography

Alen, Rupert and Dahlquist, Ana Marie, *Royal Families of Medieval Scandinavia, Flanders, and Kiev* (Kingsburg, CA: River Publications, 1997).

Ashley, Mike, *The Mammoth Book Of British Kings and Queens* (New York: Carrol and Graf Publishers, Inc., 1999).

Balslev, C.F., *Bible History* (Blair, Nebraska: Danish Lutheran Publishing House, 1918).

Capt, E. Raymond, *Gem Stones In The Breastplate, The* (Muskogee, Oklahoma: Hoffman Printing Co., 1996).

_____, *Jacob's Pillar – A Biblical Historical Study* (Muskogee, Oklahoma: Hoffman Printing Co., 1996).

_____, *Missing Links Discovered In Assyrian Tablets* (Muskogee, Oklahoma: Hoffman Printing Co., 1996).

_____, *Stonehenge and Druidism* (Muskogee, Oklahoma: Hoffman Printing Co., 1996).

_____, *Tradition of Glastonbury- The Biblical Missing Years of Christ-ANSWERED* (Muskogee, Oklahoma: Hoffman Printing Co., 1987).

Charles, R.H., *Apocalypse of Baruch, The* (Merrimac, Massachusetts: Destiny Publishers, 1988).

_____, *Book Of Enoch, The* (Oxford: Clarendon Press, 1912).

Chumney, Edward, *Seven Festivals of The Messiah, The* (Shippensburg, PA: Destiny Image Publishers Inc., 1999).

Collins, John J., *Apocalypticism In The Dead Sea Scrolls* (London, New York: Routledge, 1997).

_____, *Daniel with an Introduction to Apocalyptic Literature* (Grand Rapids, Michigan: William B. Eerdmans Publishing Company, 1984).

_____, *Scepter and the Star, The; The- Messiahs of the Dead Sea Scrolls and Other*

Ancient Literature (New York, London, Toronto, Sydney, Aukland: Doubleday, 1995).

Davidy, Yair, *Ephraim* (Jerusalem, Israel: Russel Davis Publishers, 1995).

_____, *Tribes, The* (Hebron, Israel: Russel- Davis Publishers).

Elder, Isabel Hill, *Celt, Druid, and Culdee* (Britain: Covenant Pulishing company, 1973).

Evans, H. T., *Wales and The Wars of The Roses* (United Kingdom: Alan Sutton Publishing Limited, 1995).

Gawler, J. C., *Dan- The Pioneer of Israel* (Muskogee, Oklahoma: Hoffman Printing Co., 1998).

Gordon, Cyrus, H., *Riddles in History* (New York: Crown Publishers Inc., 1974).

Gray, Andrew, *Origin and Early History of Christianity In Britain* (London: Skeffington and Son, Piccadilly, W, 1897).

Griffiths, Ralph A, *Sir Rhys Ap Thomas And His Family – A Study In The Wars Of The Roses And Early Tudor Politics* (Great Britain: Cardiff University of Wales Press, 1993).

Jowett, George F, *Drama of the Lost Disciples* (London: Covenant Publishing Co. LTD., 1996).

Koppejan, Helene, *Strange Parallel- Zebulun- Tribe of Israel* (Muskogee, Oklahoma: Artisan Publishers, 1984).

Llwelyn, Morgan, *Vikings In Ireland, The* (Dublin: The O'Brien Press, 1996).

Martinez, Florentino Garcia, *Dead Sea Scrolls Translated, The* (London, New York, E.J. Brill; Grand Rapids, William B. Eerdmans, 1996).

Rich, Bobby L., *Last Prophet, The- as described by the Dead Sea Scrolls and Biblical Scripture,* Synopsis available from http://www.panola.com/users/brich/ Internet; accessed 4 January 1998.

Rosen, Moishe, *Y'Shua* (Chicago: Moody Press, 1982).

Rossel, Seymour, *Introduction To Jewish History* (West Orange, New Jersey: Behrman House Inc., 1981).

Stough, Henry W., *Dedicated Disciples* (Muskogee Oklahoma: Artisan Publishers 1987).

Thomas, Llewellyn J., *Assyrian Invasions And Deportations of Israel* (Britain: Covenant Publishing Company, 1937).

Wilson, A.N., *Jesus- A Life* (New York: Fawcett Columbine 1993).

_____, *Paul: The Mind of The Apostle* (New York, London: W.W. Norton and Company, 1997).

Index

Printed in the United States
44074LVS00008B/4-6